CN 458.2

KT-231-080

Praise for *Toxic People*

"This may be the best book available on how to deal effectively with really difficult people. It could save your sanity and maybe even your career."

—Brian Tracy, author, *The Power of Charm*

"I guarantee you will see people you know in this book. While there are many books on leadership and personal accountability, this one truly resonates in reality and practicality. Toss the duct tape and get the book. I did."

—Jack Stroud, Executive Director,
Vorys Sater Seymour and Pease LLP

"Toxic people—how about toxic patients! As a plastic surgeon, my goal is to make people look better, but most especially feel better about themselves. Most times I succeed, but when I fail, I can encounter the toxic fumes of everyday life. Petrie Sue's book candidly reveals how toxic personalities redirect their venom into business and professional relationships, and she teaches us how to avoid letting those issues interfere with a successful outcome. A must-read for anyone in the people business."

—Martin Bell, MD, JD, North Valley
Plastic Surgery

"Petrie Sue's book makes one thing very, very clear: If you're letting toxic people make you miserable, then they're doing it with your permission. Wow! What an eye-opener!"

—Joe Calloway, best-selling author,
Work Like You're Showing Off!

"Petrie Sue's ideas on changing your responses to your personal environment so that life becomes more pleasant are practical, and they do work. I know!"
— Johanna Cogle, Principal, Queens
Academic Group, Auckland, New Zealand

"You will never again need to think, 'How do I handle this situation?' Petrie Sue's book provides easy-to-remember specific solutions for dealing with all types of negative or stressful people. Her formula of TLC—take it, leave it, or change it—can improve your professional and personal life forever. Don't let deadly toxic people contaminate you anymore."
— Tracee Lee Curtis, CFA, CFP

"Rather than simply suffering the consequences, read this practical book and learn specific, sane skills you can use to deal positively and effectively with toxic people."
— Mark Sanborn, author, *The Fred Factor*
and *You Don't Need a Title to Be a Leader*

"Freedom from conflict will never happen *unless* you buy and read Petrie Sue's new book, *Toxic People*. It's loaded with practical, entertaining ideas to turn those toxic relationships into productive ones."
— Dr. Tony Alessandra, best-selling author,
The Platinum Rule and *Charisma*

TOXIC PEOPLE

TOXIC PEOPLE

DECONTAMINATE DIFFICULT PEOPLE AT WORK

WITHOUT USING WEAPONS OR DUCT TAPE

MARSHA PETRIE SUE

John Wiley & Sons, Inc.

Published by John Wiley & Sons, Inc., Hoboken, New Jersey.
Published simultaneously in Canada.

Wiley Bicentennial Logo: Richard J. Pacifico.

For general information on our other products and services or for technical support, please contact our Customer Care Department within the United States at (800) 762-2974, outside the United States at (317) 572-3993 or fax (317) 572-4002.

Wiley also publishes its books in a variety of electronic formats. Some content that appears in print may not be available in electronic books. For more information about Wiley products, visit our web site at www.wiley.com.

Library of Congress Cataloging-in-Publication Data:

ISBN 978-0-470-14768-9

Printed in the United States of America.
10 9 8 7 6 5 4 3 2 1

Contents

Contents

Preface

Caution: Expect discomfort while reading this book — don't just enjoy it. This is the only life you have, so you might as well learn how to manage people who create perplexity, puzzlement, and pandemonium. You know the ones — Toxic People!

My approach to dealing with difficult people, poor communications, and conflict is one that aims to be unique, funny, and based on common sense. And this may tick you off, because my approach is not so much about the difficult person as it is about *you*.

If you are tired of people, including yourself, not taking personal responsibility for their choices, then this is the book for you. If you are sick of one person or a few people in your group — the minority — ruling the majority, then you are reading the right book.

If you want to have the skills to manage unacceptable behavior in the workplace, welcome. I decided that life is just too short to let people upset me, get my goat, or make me mad. Whether you are a leader or not, this is a no-fluff, no-nonsense approach to identifying and managing anyone who drives you nuts! Using weapons and duct tape is often tempting, but after being sent to charm school twice in my corporate career, I realized this is not the best approach! What weapons are you using now with Toxic People? Do you carry a roll of duct tape with you just to shut them up? Or maybe you use the tape over your ears because you are fed up with listening to them.

First step: Stop pointing a finger at other people and how awful they are. There are reasons you are not winning the blame game. Take a long, hard look in the mirror at the person you have become.

If you don't agree with the ideas you find here, give this book to someone who gets it—someone who is ready to eliminate, not just reduce, the power of all those people who tend to tick you off or make you crazy!

So many of us complain about this person or that person, this toxic group or that difficult boss. However, it's not about other people. It is truly all about us and how we choose to manage ourselves and the situation.

You will learn how to take the offensive against the "yes" people, "no" people, gripers, snipers, dictators, experts, and all the other characters you confront every day. Or you might label them as Steamrollers, Zipper Lips, Backstabbers, Know-It-Alls, Needy Weenies, and the ultimate pain—Whine and Cheesers! You have to learn how to identify the behaviors, the payoffs for them, approaches to use, and what methods to avoid.

Toxic People often make you question your own capabilities and sanity. You have to get a grip on survival tactics that work. You'll be amazed at how easily you can turn an ugly situation into a tolerable event.

Gain the self-confidence and know-how you need to manage every problem and every difficult person in your life.

Preface

Learn how Toxic People think and why they choose to be toxic. Then learn what you can do immediately to change the negative outcomes you typically get.

You must understand that you can only turn to yourself to manage conflict, anger, and poor interpersonal relations. Having the skills and applying them is your responsibility. Personal accountability is the real key. Choose to take control of Toxic People, and don't allow them to control you.

The style of this book is focused. The ideas are presented with humor and real-life applications that make it easy for you to remember and use the techniques presented.

Many business books on the market today give people communication tools, but using them is only half of the way to decontaminate Toxic People. Communicating is only part of the story. My belief is that you have to look in the mirror first, and change yourself. Only then are you ready to manage the Toxic People in your life.

Businesspeople have to stop pointing a finger at someone else. *You* need to change yourself, your communications, and your approach. You have to stop relying on the buzzword of the day or the latest consultancy theory. Then, and only then, will you be able to really change your environment, create high morale, and develop successful work groups.

I realized this long ago in my corporate life and had to learn new strategies to manage all the jerks who wandered the sacred halls of my business life. Notice the word *learn*. Figuring out that I was not anointed with these skills was a huge "aha" for me. Stop thinking, "Well, my company won't send me for training." You are right. I had to seek out the appropriate learning mode for me.

Preface

The silos of silence and isolation must be broken down. Poor behavior cannot be tolerated, and internal fighting must stop. Toxic People must be decontaminated!

If you're tired of the effects that Toxic People and toxic environments have on your personal and professional life, stop complaining and get busy. Everything you need to decontaminate the folks and situations that are toxic to you is presented on the pages that follow. Don't just read them. Read them and decide how to adapt them to fit your style and situation. Then put them into practice and pay attention to the results you get.

Acknowledgments

My dad always taught me that I didn't have to know how to do everything on my own and emphasized the need to find the right resources. I certainly learned that lesson and would like to thank those resources, friends, and colleagues who helped me with *Toxic People*.

First, thanks to all the Toxic People in my life. You gave me stories to share in this book, and you helped me learn how to manage my own behavior and not give in to your upsetting behavior.

To Kurt Boxdorfer and Jan Olsen-Beeso, who do so much to keep my web site and technology working, and Janita Cooper for her guidance on my product development.

To Rosalie Hydock, PhD, who helped me with the sophisticated behavioral perspectives while not stripping my voice from the writing. Linda Norman, Karen Gridley, and Toni Farrar dotted the i's and crossed the t's with their proofreading extraordinaire.

A huge thank-you to the extraordinary staff at John Wiley & Sons for helping me with absolutely everything. Your quick response to my questions, whether simple or complex, was terrific.

To the Wingets, who are always there to help me succeed. Rose Mary, with her editing capabilities and publishing experience, polished the message and flow. Larry, the author of two best-selling books (*Shut Up, Stop Whining, and Get a Life* and *It's Called Work for a Reason*) and A&E TV host of *Big Spender*,

Acknowledgments

always takes the time to review anything I ask and offer input and changes that take me to the next level.

And to my husband, Al Sue, for his amazing support and flexibility.

Thanks to everyone else who helped. Your assistance, support, experience, and guidance are appreciated more than you will ever know.

TOXIC PEOPLE

CHAPTER 1

A Hair in
Your Biscuit

I I I

There have been people put on this earth to push your buttons,
tick you off, and suck the life out of you. You know who they
are. If you are tired of being contaminated by these Toxic People,
read on.

*I was a sales manager for a Fortune 100 company and had just made
the decision to reinvent myself. Watching successful people and how
they build relationships seemed to be the ticket, and I had just heard
the statement "Treat people as you want to be treated." Monday morning I entered the building smiling and immediately ran into my boss,
who said (her actual words, so don't blame me!) "What are you so
f___ing happy about? You usually look like you found a hair in your
biscuit or that somebody peed in your coffee."*

Lovely. I immediately knew I was on the right track, because it

1

*really was a pain to work for her. The happier I got, the crappier she
got. Perfect. My emphasis on being positive got me promoted within
a short time, and her attitude led to an eventual ride on the prover-
bial broomstick into the sunset.*

You have several choices when thinking about coping strategies. These include hating the Toxic People, quitting your job, or
just plain copping out. In messy interactions, you unwittingly promote the behavior you don't want mainly because the mind is lazy
and you want an easy fix. There is no easy way to cope, however, so
you need to consider dumping your current behaviors and learning new approaches. You need to move from emotional reaction to
effective action. This means old skills must be tossed and new ones
learned and practiced. Translation: no more excuses!

Have you ever said:

"I'm so mad I can't see straight."

"They make me so angry!"

"Who do they think they are?"

"They just don't know who they are messing with!"

"They really tick me off! I'll get them!!"

These words are an admission that the other person is controlling you. Is that what you really want? If your answer to this question is "Sure" or "Sometimes," stop reading, and give this book to
someone who *does* want to change. And believe me, some people
just give anger management lip service. They really don't want the
situation to change.

Here is the hard reality. If you have bad relationships, it's your

---

PLEDGE

I, _____ [your name], promise that I will identify toxic behavior, use new skills in my approach, and *never* use excuses again. I have the strength and fortitude to continue to practice, even after I have failed. I am never the Toxic Person. I pledge to stay calm and keep my temper. I promise never to take a Toxic Person's behavior personally or to seek retribution. I know how to keep my power by maintaining control. I create my own environment that nurtures my success. I am the master of my future, my stress level, and my own behavior.

---

fault. If you have poor outcomes, you created them. You must take personal responsibility for every choice and outcome in your life.

If you would like the pledge e-mailed to you, please send your message to Information@MarshaPetrieSue.com. It would make a great screen saver!

Try a Little TLC—Take It, Leave It, or Change It

You always have choices when deciding what to do in a toxic situation. When you are stuck in a rut and feel you have nowhere to turn, stop and question yourself. "Do I choose to take it, leave it, or change it? What's my plan?"

When you feel buried and overwhelmed, pull yourself up by the bootstraps and say, "Okay, I have three choices. I can take it, leave it, or change it. What's my plan?" Stop using victim talk such as, "I can't," "I won't be able to," or "It will never work." You've used this strategy in the past and developed it into a habit. Here is the TLC (Take it. Leave it. Change it.) for making better choices:

1. *Take it.* When you accept events as they are in the moment, you send a message to yourself that it is okay for right now—maybe not perfect, but livable. The situation is not creating tremendous stress or discomfort. You know this state is temporary. With focus, goals, and planning, the future will be different. Let's face it, though; sometimes the situation isn't temporary, and it is not moderate, but you decide to take it, take it, and take it until you hate everyone at work, including yourself. Learn when it's time to let go. Get a grip and have a plan.

2. *Leave it.* The most difficult decision you face is when you reject the situation and are forced to step out of your comfort zone. This can appear as a great and overwhelming risk. This is when you say, "I'm not going to accept it the way it is, and I know I can't change it, so I'm leaving." Have you left a job or relationship because you couldn't take it any longer? This was your choice to leave. You read and hear story after story of people being forced to move on to a new job, a new location, or a new company and actually coming out ahead. A good example would be losing a client, only to have an even better new customer appear. No risk, no reward.

3. *Change it.* Making a change may appear to be difficult and even overwhelming because it takes you to a place you've never been. However, managing the unknown can be as

easy as changing your perspective, your opinion, or your attitude. Other times you have to negotiate and dig to get what you want. Deciding to change means tackling what is going on *right now* for the sake of building something better *later*. It takes work to identify what you need. It takes courage to ask for what you want. Remember, if you can't accept it and don't want to leave it, then working for change is the only remaining option. You always have options. You can choose to change it or choose not to change it. It's not that you can't!

Use this TLC approach whether the hair in your biscuit is a person or an annoying situation. When others try to involve you in their problem, create your own environment—and a better outcome—by calmly using the TLC approach.

External Use of TLC

The next time your Toxic Person comes up to you complaining, "You won't believe what happened," and then rants on and on about some problem, you respectfully interrupt and say, "You know what I've learned? I've learned that I always have three choices. I can take it, leave it, or change it." (Explain each of these choices.) "So what's your plan?" Notice the use of "I" language rather than "you" language. This demonstrates your personal accountability instead of pointing a finger at the other person, and you become a role model.

The Toxic Person may go on with, "Well, you know I have no control." Again, you respectfully interrupt and say, with the same graciousness you used before, "You know what I've learned? I've learned that I have three choices. I can take it, leave it, or change it. So what's your plan?"

The other person then chimes in with, "Well, it's a jungle out there." Again you respond, "You know what I've learned? I've learned that I have three choices. I can take it, leave it, or change it. So what's your plan?"

You probably are not going to change anyone, but these Toxic People will leave you alone and go suck the life out of someone else, because you are not buying into their behavior. This technique of making the same statement repeatedly is called the *broken record* technique. Keep repeating the same thing using the same tone, pleasantries, and focus. If you are a parent, I'll bet you use it with your children. You will find out that it is effective at work as well!

Dear Marsha,

I heard you on our monthly learning session. I am a consultant with a multilevel marketer (MLM) and am working to be promoted. I listen to positive, self-affirming information every day. Your idea of the TLC approach is brilliant!

Here is my main problem. I talk to one of my down-line people, Marcia, every day. She is the most negative person I know. She constantly complains about how she has too few shows, has exhausted her list of contacts, has too much paperwork, and so on. Everything in her life is a complaint, and of course nothing is ever her fault. She plays the blame game. I loved your advice about TLC and want to use it with her. I am worried about her response. Do you have any advice for me? She really could be a great producer. I try to help her in many ways, and nothing is ever enough. She absolutely does not buy into my way of thinking. You are what you think about.

Thanks for reading my message and for any advice you can give.

Diane

Here is the response from me, the Decontaminator of Toxic People:

Great to hear from you! Why do you worry about her response? Will it make her more negative? When you approach her using the TLC, you are not being emotional, judgmental, or abrasive. You are just giving her your point of view. When you ask her, "So what's your plan?," you are putting the ball in her court.

I also think it is really great to ask negative people whether they just want you to listen or they are looking for solutions. If they are just wanting me to listen, I will say something like, "Okay, I have only two minutes" (or whatever time I want to give them), and if they say they need more, I will tell them that I'm trying hard to stay positive. Then I will go into the TLC! Does this help?

Thanks for using "Ask Marsha" from the web site, and I look forward to hearing from you!

Marsha

The TLC approach works with any Toxic Person. It is also important to identify which toxic type you are dealing with and then tailor the approach to what works best with that type! Remember: They can't get you unless you let them! Learn to identify which toxic type they are, and then you can choose the best approach. In this book, six types of Toxic People are identified, and you will learn how to spot them, manage the situation, and keep yourself sane.

Chapter 3—The Steamroller: bully, aggressor, always right.

Chapter 4—The Zipper Lip: clam, no response.

Chapter 5—The Backstabber: snake in a suit, psychopath.

Chapter 6—The Know-It-All: arrogant expert, always right.

Chapter 7—The Needy Weenie: wimp, worrywart.

Chapter 8—The Whine and Cheeser: chronic complainer, always negative.

You can probably guess the behaviors associated with each of these, and you may even have names you could attach. Understanding the message they send, how *you* perceive it, and why they choose the behavior is all part of the decontamination process. Each of these Toxic People types will be reviewed in detail.

Liar Liar, Pants on Fire

Liars can be the hair in your biscuit. J.J. Newberry was a trained federal agent, skilled in the art of deception detection. So when a witness to a shooting sat in front of him and tried to tell him that when she heard gunshots she didn't look, she just ran, he could tell she was lying. How did Newberry reach this conclusion? By recognizing telltale signs that a person isn't being honest, like inconsistencies in a story, behavior that is different from a person's norm, or too much detail in an explanation. In this case, her described behavior didn't match what people typically do when a sound startles them. From birth, individuals with normal hearing will react by immediately turning in the direction of the sound.

While using these signs to catch a liar takes extensive training and practice, it's no longer only for authorities like Newberry. Now you can become good at identifying dishonesty, and it's not as hard as you might think. Here are 10 tips.

LOOK FOR INCONSISTENCIES

Listen for inconsistencies in what people are saying. This means you have to really hear their message. Newberry was questioning a woman who said she ran and hid after hearing gunshots—without looking—and Newberry saw the inconsistency immediately.

"There was something that just didn't fit," says Newberry. "She heard gunshots, but she didn't look? I knew that was inconsistent with how a person would respond to a situation like that." So, when she wasn't paying attention, he banged on the table. She looked right at him. "When a person hears a noise, it's a natural reaction to look toward it," Newberry said. "I knew she heard those gunshots, looked in the direction from which they came, saw the shooter, and *then* ran." Sure enough, he was right.

He knew her story was illogical. You need to look for inconsistencies if you think someone is not being truthful. Is there anything that just doesn't fit? The key here is to pay attention to what they are saying rather than trying to figure out what you will say next. (More on listening in Chapter 11, "Listen Up!")

ASK THE UNEXPECTED

Did you know that approximately 4 percent of people are accomplished liars? To catch them, you have to be more clever than they are. What would be great is to have a lie-o-meter or a Pinocchio-reader ring. Since neither of these is available, you have to use your questioning and observational skills.

Use your eyes and watch them carefully. When they least expect it, shift the conversation with a question they do not anticipate and listen for their response. Have you tripped them up? Are they stammering? Do they lose eye contact? Watch their body language, and if they start to lean or step back, this can be a good indicator. Excessive eye blinking is also a sign. (But beware—they may just be nervous.) If you do detect a combination of these peculiarities, you may have caught them in a lie!

DOES THEIR BEHAVIOR CHANGE?

When you know someone, be alert for changes in behavior. If someone who is generally calm all of a sudden becomes fidgety, this is a red flag that sends you a message of behavioral change. Or perhaps someone who usually is very quick-paced and talks at a rapid rate suddenly appears to be moving more slowly and their speech pattern slows down.

"One of the most important indicators of dishonesty is changes in behavior," says Maureen O'Sullivan, PhD, a professor of psychology at the University of San Francisco. "You want to pay attention to someone who is generally anxious but now looks calm, or someone who is generally calm but now looks anxious."

The trick is to gauge their behavior against a baseline. Is their behavior deviating from how they would normally act? If it is, that could mean something is up.

LOOK FOR INSINCERE EMOTIONS

Have you ever faked a smile? Of course you have! Most people can't fake a smile convincingly. You have detected a fake smile when the timing was wrong, the smile was held too long, or it was incongruent with the situation. O'Sullivan says, "Maybe it will be a combination of an angry face with a smile; you can tell because their lips are smaller and less full than in a sincere smile." These fake emotions are a good indicator that something has gone amiss.

PAY ATTENTION TO GUT REACTIONS

Your gut reaction is a result of all the experiences you have had. This includes the good, the bad, and the ugly. When you hear those voices in your head warning, "Beware!," listen to them. Events and people in your past have done or said something memorable that became a frame of reference for you. When all these frames become a reel of film, they speak in the form of gut reaction or intuition.

> Beatrice was an excellent caregiver, and Jeff's mom, Sophia, always looked forward to her scheduled time. Christmas Eve was traditionally a family event with neighbors dropping into Sophia's home to savor homemade cookies and champagne. Beatrice surprised Jeff by staying past her scheduled time. Her behavior was also a shock, as she imbibed too much and became quite different. She apologized the next day, and Jeff let it pass. However, his gut told him to beware.
>
> Jeff started paying closer attention to Beatrice's behavior. About

11

two months later, he was notified that she had lied and had not taken care of Mom for an entire day—leaving Sophia alone! The service that employed Beatrice was very apologetic and asked Jeff what he wanted to do. Their recommendation was to terminate her. Although difficult to do, Jeff knew firing her was appropriate.

While you might not know what it is you're seeing when you think someone isn't being honest and you might attribute it to suspicion or instinct, a scientist would be able to pinpoint it exactly, which leads us to the next tip.

WATCH FOR MICROEXPRESSIONS

When you have a gut feeling, Paul Ekman, PhD, a renowned expert in lie detection, sees microexpressions. "A microexpression is a very brief expression, usually about a 25th of a second, that is always a concealed emotion," says Ekman.

When someone is acting happy but in actuality is upset about something, the true emotion is revealed in a flash on the face. Whether the concealed emotion is fear, anger, happiness, or jealousy, that feeling will appear on the face and be gone in the blink of an eye. The trick is for you to see it on other people.

"Almost everyone—99 percent of those we've tested in about 10,000 people—won't see the microexpressions," says Ekman. "But it can be taught."

In fact, in less than an hour, the average person can learn to see microexpressions. Develop this skill and you will have a powerful tool for interacting with others. Google Microexpressions for more information.

LOOK FOR CONTRADICTIONS

Do their words match their facial expressions and their postures? Paying attention will help you to identify contradictions and incongruities. Watch and listen carefully to a Toxic Person.

Your tendency is to play the mental terrorism game and think about all the ways you are going to get back at them. Sometimes when people are falsely saying, "Yes, *she's* the one who lied," they will, without knowing it, make a slight head shake "no." That subtle gesture contradicts what they're saying in words.

These contradictions, explains Ekman, can be between the voice and the words, the gesture and the voice, the gesture and the words, or the facial expression and the words. When you see a contradiction, watch out. Something isn't quite adding up. They could be lying.

NOTICE A SENSE OF UNEASE

You can see untruthful people beginning to squirm. Watch their breathing. Are their shoulders moving up and down more than usual? If so, they are breathing shallowly, probably because of nervousness. Licking the lips too much, fidgeting, sweating, shifting from foot to foot, all can be signs of anxiety and uneasiness. You have to pay attention to the other person, not yourself!

Listen for vocal interjections. Too many "um's," "uh's," or "you know's" can be indicators that they are searching for more words to cover up their lies.

BEWARE OF TOO MUCH DETAIL

You have heard children include extra detail to cover their tracks and lies. Adults also do this when lying, but they are much more clever about it. Wordiness may be a behavioral and vocal trait, though, so beware of jumping to conclusions. In most cases, however, it is not and is used when people want to fill the airspace for their own reasons. Too much detail could mean they've put a lot of thought into how they're going to get out of a situation and they've constructed a complicated lie as a solution.

DON'T IGNORE THE TRUTH

When the environment is toxic, you must be aware of when someone is *telling the truth*. Experience and the negative frames of reference can begin to jaundice you into thinking there is no truth. While it sounds contradictory, finding the truth buried under a lie can sometimes help reveal the answer to an important question: Why is a person lying?

■ ■ ■

These 10 truth tips all help detect deception. What they don't do is tell you why a person is lying and what the lie means.

This is where your experience and training in human behavior will help you understand if emotions are concealed. When you think someone is lying, you have to either know the person well enough to understand why they might lie, or be a people expert. Learn to speed-read people, their expressions, and their approaches. Make it more about them and less about you. I believe that in today's society most people are so focused on themselves that they don't function well in any situation, especially difficult ones.

Extra Tip: Be Trusting

The dictionary defines *trust* as confidence in and reliance on good qualities, especially fairness, truth, honor, or ability.

Is this you 100 percent of the time? We have the responsibility to take good care of ourselves and others. In general, we have a choice about which stance we take in life. Choose suspicion, and life is not going to be particularly pleasant, but we won't be misled very often. If we take a trusting stance, life is going to be a lot more pleasant, but sometimes we are going to be taken in.

My mom took the suspicion route and my dad took the trusting stance. I remember that I couldn't play with Dougie, our next-door neighbor, because my mom said Dougie had "sneaky eyes." So of course I started looking for sneaky-eyed people. The good news was that my dad's approach was to trust everyone unless they "did you wrong." Dad always said, "Lie to me once, shame on you. Lie to me twice, shame on me." So at least I was raised with a little balance.

How about you? What were the lessons you learned about trust? How do you apply them in your life? How do you apply them in toxic situations?

A business colleague sent me this example. In the real world, trust is the cornerstone of a successful long-term business relationship.

Clive, one of my vendors, began talking directly to one of my long-term customers, a woman named Jamie. I was quite surprised, because he had never before circumvented our company and approached our clients directly. I had already suggested some of his products to Jamie.

Clive made promises to her that I knew could not be kept and gave Jamie bad information about our pricing. He took her business from us and dealt with her directly.

Due to Clive's lies, I lost a great client, and I really thought there was no way to win her back. I didn't want to look like a weak link or come off like sour grapes. So, I studied various approaches and found a very useful communication model that I used.

Here's how I decided to approach Jamie. I said, "I am honored to be part of your supply chain. We have both enjoyed a great working relationship. My concern is that you have accurate data that allows you to make decisions with information that is correct."

I continued, "Clive gave you some background information about my business and company practices that I would like to correct. Do you want me to share those details with you now, or should we invite Clive to join us so you can hear the entire story?"

My goal was to open Jamie's mind, voice my concern, and provide correct information. The statement of the problem was brief, and I offered Jamie two choices. She was able to choose and felt ownership in the situation. We did win her business back!

Toxic People abound in today's business environment and provide that hair in your biscuit. Your challenge is to dump old approaches and create new skills that will effectively help you succeed. Evaluating each situation and being comfortable with your approach to move forward will make every situation easier to handle.

CHAPTER 2

Doesn't Work
Well with Others

▮ ▮ ▮

You can no longer avoid responsibility for your conflicts, bad relationships, or how people treat you. I know you are confronted with injustices that you cannot change. Favoritism, privileges not deserved, and stupid people who tick you off permeate your work environment. If you believe the universe should give you a fair break, say "Amen!"

If you don't work well with others, these six rules can help you change. If you work with people who don't work well with you, these will help you stay sane.

Don't Try to Change People

The only person you can change is yourself. Constantly review and polish the skills you know work. If you don't have the skills, attend a seminar, read a book, download information to your iPod, or do something else that will help you acquire them. Visit my web site at www.MarshaPetrieSue.com, where you will find tons of information to help you be better at managing your problems.

> *Lori hired Geoff on the recommendation of a friend. Geoff was likable and well received by the sales group and by the clients. The only issue that Lori was warned about was his challenge with time management. After just one month, the complaints from clients and the administration began to flood in about his missed appointments, improperly completed contracts, unreturned phone calls, and more. Geoff admitted to his problem and promised to improve.*
>
> *His second month was not much better, so Lori decided to send him to a time management class. Geoff was thrilled that she was helping him with this ongoing problem. The class provided excellent resources and ideas, including individual coaching from the trainer for six months. The first week after the class was fabulous, and Lori congratulated him on improving his paperwork flow and general follow-up.*
>
> *Halfway into the following week, Geoff fell off the wagon and went back to his old habits. Lori warned him that he had one month to resolve these issues or he would be released from employment. Lori was grateful that the human resources department had set up a six-month trial employment period so any new hire who didn't work out could be released. And that is what Lori had to do. Geoff was not surprised at all and said, "Oh, well. It's just too difficult to change. I don't want to work that hard."*

Quit Knee-Jerking

Notice that *knee-jerking* contains the word *jerk*? In my opinion, if you are knee-jerking, you're the jerk and you will get jerky outcomes! You have to learn the difference between *responding* to Toxic People and reacting to them. Responding is learned, and reacting is knee-jerk. Choosing to react contaminates situations, and conflict is the result. Do you want to give your control and power to other people? When you use an inappropriate approach, you are reacting without thinking; your mission will be accomplished, but it won't be a positive one. Remember that reacting without thinking is when you are hijacked by mental terrorism.

Responding is taking the communication and mental tools you know and applying them to a situation. My father said to me, "Put your mind in gear before running off at the mouth." It's too bad it took me so long to learn how to do it. How about you? Do you *always* have your mind in gear, or do you knee-jerk?

Control Ugly Outcomes

Okay—someone ticks you off. You can either knee-jerk or use a more mature approach of digging deeper and finding out where *they* are coming from. Choose to knee-jerk and you will have anger, conflict, and problems. Choose maturity and skill, and you will manage the Toxic Person and situation effectively. Just try it. No excuses.

IN YOUR FACE

Faye's boss approached her again with his finger pointed in her face, screaming, "And if you can't do it, I'll find someone who can!" She jumped to his commands, worked too many hours, and never seemed to satisfy his expectations. Faye had to face the fact that her boss was a Toxic Person. When she began asking him to define the outcomes he expected, he became louder and crazier. Her stomach hurt, and she had terrible headaches and couldn't sleep.

So, Faye made a decision. She evaluated her talents, revised her re-sume, and put the word out that she was interested in a change. Faye networked diligently. She had a mini makeover and updated her busi-ness look. A Fortune 100 company heard through the grapevine that she was looking. After a series of interviews, she was hired. She never once said that she had worked for a Toxic Person. She focused on what she really wanted: to be able to use her talents to help a company be-come even more successful and to be appreciated for her contributions. Her strategic efforts got her the job of her dreams. In her new position her health improved, because her toxic work situation was what had been making her sick.

Faye's friend Mark was in a similar position. He had less geo-graphical flexibility and didn't want to move, so he networked within his company and nearby. Before long, another department hired Mark because he was able to package and market himself in a posi-tive way.

Both Faye and Mark took charge of their situations and used their skills to move forward.

Dump the "Yabit Habit"

How do you feel when you make a comment or suggestion to someone and they say, "Yes, but . . ."? These two words discount everything previously said, and conflict can occur. Start listening for these words, because they are commonly used by Toxic People.

"Yes, but . . ." "Yeah, but . . ." "Yah, but . . ." "Ya, but . . ." "Ya, bit . . ." "Yabit . . ."

Enter the Yabit Habit. Replace "Yes, but . . ." with "However" or "And." "Yes, but . . ." negates what the other person has said and can jump-start toxicity in them and for the relationship. "Yes, but . . ." said repeatedly leads to the Yabit Habit.

I HATE MY JOB

Bob would wake up in the morning with the voice in his head saying, "I hate my job." He had been with the same company for many years and was just holding out for retirement. He hated his responsibilities, his boss was a toad, and his team was too gung ho. His teammates would reproach him for not carrying his load, and he would say, "Yes, but I've been here for 27 years and it is time for me to relax." The team would try to reason with him about his lack of effort and he would Yabit them: "Yes, but I've worked my tail off, and the company should let me slide for the next couple of years."

Bob's wife, Judy, was concerned about him. She would often suggest that he take up a hobby and Bob would respond, "Yes, but if I do that I'll be too tired to work," or the ever-popular "Yes, but I don't have enough energy now to even play golf with my buddies." So Bob's work ethic was awful, his work product was sacrificed, and guess what happened? The company outsourced his job overseas and Bob was laid off. He Yabited himself into unemployment.

I LOVE MY JOB

Karol has been in banking ever since graduating from college. She quickly recognized that spending her career as a teller was not what she wanted. She identified the type of work she was attracted to, then found a mentor to help her understand the kind of education she needed. Randy, her mentor, was wonderful and guided her through the banking maze. Each time a bank Karol worked for merged with another, Karol's job would be in jeopardy because of job redundancy. In the 20 years of her career, she has been laid off three times. Every time one bank bought out another, she

21

made the choice to put a positive spin on the merger and welcomed the opportunity to move up to an even better banking position. Randy has remained a good friend and mentor. Her connection with him, as well as her focused choices, allowed her to not become a victim of circumstance.

Watch Your Mouth

Stop saying, "Do you understand?" How do you feel when someone says this to you? Does the mental terrorism in your own head kick in? Do you say to yourself, "Well, do you think I'm an idiot? Of course I understand!" Enter toxicity. Change this question to "I want to make sure I was clear. Would you please tell me what you heard in your own words?" or something to that effect. Be careful not to sound condescending. Use open body language—no crossed arms. Avoid sarcasm, and deliver your message with consideration and graciousness.

WELL, DO YOU UNDERSTAND?

With her arms folded, May, the team lead, entered the project planning session and gave each seated participant a short memo outlining an additional client request. She requested they read the memo, and each diligently did so. Then she asked condescendingly, "Do you understand?" The group all silently nodded and waited for May to leave. They then spent the next half hour discussing her arrogance and rudeness. Simply rephrasing the question and altering her body language would have helped the team get on with integrating the client's request into the project. What a waste of time and energy when people don't look at better approaches. May had a hard time working well with others.

Attitude Does Count

If you look at life through a negative lens, I can guarantee negative outcomes. You really do become what you think about. I made a choice some time ago to be positive—not to be a Pollyanna but to be realistic. My discovery was that Toxic People really don't like being around positive people, because positive people have tools to manage their ugly behavior. Negative people don't. Remember that a positive attitude may not solve all your problems, but it will annoy enough people to make it worth the effort.

What puts you in the toxic frame of mind? What do you really need to do when you go there mentally? You probably perceive yourself as always getting the middle seat—that place in life where you've got a meanie on one side and a real jerk on the other. You know how to solve the problem: Decide not to play their game. Start changing your focus today, and you will be amazed how Toxic People lose the game.

■ *Create pleasant memories.* Set yourself up for happiness by planning events that you know will have happy endings. Instead of maintaining a pattern of defeat and ugliness, you begin to see things in a more positive light. My belief is that you actually train yourself how to enjoy the present and create your future.

■ *Relish every day.* Learn to celebrate small things and combat sameness. Concentrate on staying pleasant, and learn to be grateful. Don't get caught up in an excess of anything—eating, sleeping, exercising, working, shopping, or anything else.

■ *See friends and make connections.* Go out of your way, right now, to send an e-mail or text message to someone you care for and haven't connected with in a while. Individuals who are connected tend to be more emotionally resilient. Just knowing you have support makes it easier to tolerate life's little disasters.

■ *Stay out of heavy traffic,* because it just makes you realize your lack of control. Like life, sometimes you have to find a new route. This mentally places you in control, and you are in for a more pleasant ride.

■ *Limit your options*; otherwise your mind stimulates debate. There are just too many choices in life. Too many choices equals using your limited time and energy on trivial decisions. Instead of reading every item on the six-page restaurant menu, know what you want before you arrive. When I go out for a routine lunch, for example, I narrow it down by knowing I'll order some salad that has chicken in it. Then I can focus on my company and any business or socializing.

■ *Enjoy what you do*—you own your career. You choose the job. Are you upset about some event at work? Be grateful you have a job, and create an environment of success for yourself.

■ *Don't follow the herd.* Don't talk, dress, or act like the rest of the people, but stay within your own comfort zone.

■ *Use humor.* Lighten up. You take yourself way too seriously. Laugh more.

■ *Learn from your mistakes.* Get over them and move on.

■ *Form your own opinions.* Think for yourself. Don't take what you read in the newspaper, see on television, hear on the radio, or Google on the Internet as gospel. And don't conform to someone else's thinking just to have them like you.

▌ *Play to win.* Success, by your own definition, is a critical component for you to have a happy life, build good relationships, and die satisfied with the person you have chosen to be. You are 100 percent in control.

There are always people judging you, so remember the other side of toxic behavior and how people view you. How do you think you are perceived at work? Do you work well with others? Play by the rules, and you will win the game!

CHAPTER 3

The Steamroller

■ ■ ■

Take I: How They Sound

Late as usual! Jerry huffed into the meeting, dramatically pulled out the large leather chair, and spread his papers over his allotted space at the conference table. After a quick glance at the agenda he had approved, he loudly said, "Morgan, I've already told you not to distribute the agenda before I arrive. Do I need to remind you again? Or perhaps I should get you, my assistant, a keeper."

Morgan sheepishly explained that the group had requested the agendas so they could begin the meeting to save time. Pounding on the table, Jerry bellowed, "I buy everyone's time, and I will determine how it is used!" Not surprisingly, Jerry's brainstorming meeting was unsuccessful, because everyone was too terrified to speak.

So, what would you do in this situation? Would you know how to identify the kind of Toxic Person depicted in this example? Could you respond appropriately to create a more productive environment?

Names Will Never Hurt Me

Steamrollers, like Jerry, can also be known as exploders, dominators, tyrants, dictators, bullies, autocrats, oppressors, persecutors, or tormenters. We all have had at least one of these in our lives as an authoritative parent, boss, colleague, or friend. They are not much fun to be around.

What to Look For

Steamrollers are very intimidating. Their favorite stance is to get control by putting others down, and they do this very subtly. They like to rule from a command post and attack without warning so they are in the power position. Typically, they are fast to attack and quick to anger. Being judgmental is part of the package, and they love to say no to changes they haven't initiated, because that way they keep control of the power. Listening to new ideas and suggestions for the implementation of new and innovative processes does not play well because of Steamrollers' rigidity. When they are angered, they are loud and their volume is usually elevated to command attention.

The Message the Steamroller Sends

Steamrollers want you to interpret their messages in ways that will further intimidate you and make you question your approach to them. This is what they want you to hear:

"Don't expect me to be part of the charm brigade."

"I won't give you a fair break no matter how hard you try."

"Give in to me and I won't hurt you."

"Let me have my own way or I will humiliate you and carry a grudge."

"Defer to me and I'll pretend I like you."

"If you want to be criticized, ask me to do something."

"Do not arouse me—I'll attack."

The Payoff for the Steamroller's Toxic Behavior

Steamrollers have figured out that this surly behavior works, and they really don't care if they are liked. They maintain control and power by bullying people. Since most people fear them, communications from others are limited and the Steamrollers don't have to take responsibility. They like being feared because people leave them alone.

Survival Tactics

Learn what communication skills and approaches work in dealing with Steamrollers. Listen and be patient. When you don't get the outcomes you want, understand why and what skill you will polish and improve. Train yourself to be firm and direct while maintaining graciousness.

Don't give a knee-jerk response or react inappropriately. Steamrollers are much more clever than you and will triumph every time. When they are on the path of confrontation, wait, pause, and think. And remember—don't attack. They are better at it than you are, and they have had more practice.

Use their names to get their attention. Interestingly, we all hear our own name over anything else said. Maintain direct eye contact without glaring or giving them a surly look.

You must stay calm. Focus on staying composed by monitoring your tone and volume. Begin by deep breathing to get the oxygen surging from the lower part of your lungs to your brain. When Steamrollers attack, you will have a tendency to revert to the fight-or-flight response—wanting to hit them or run away.

Concentrate on the words you should be using. This simple step will keep you focused and using the strategic part of your brain rather than being entwined in the mental terrorist part of your thinking. Watch your self-talk, because the minute you start saying to yourself, "Well, here we go again. I guess they really are better than I am, so I will just give up," that's when you do. When you get angry, you are giving your power up to the Steamrollers, and that is just what they want. You will rarely win with them.

> *Mabel knew what she wanted: success and control at any price. She expected her management team to be in early for her leadership meetings. She had no tolerance for child-care issues or illness. If she wanted something completed, she had no problem in requiring that the work be taken home. A few people learned from her because she was very successful in turning around broken departments and building profits, but these people had to have very tough skins. She intimidated much of the staff.*

What would you do in this situation? What would your plan be?

Does your Steamroller totally control meetings? Having meeting ground rules (outlined in Chapter 4) is an excellent way to better manage a group setting that includes this upsetting kind of behavior. One ground rule to add is the time-out. If you work with someone who really knows how to push your buttons, say that you are working on being a better communicator and need the person's help. Continue by explaining, "I want to make sure I am responding appropriately, so when I am not able to do this, I will call a time-out. My promise is that I will come back to you within 24 hours" — or whatever time period is appropriate — "and give you my comments and input. This will save you time and relay better information to you." Play with the words and outline a couple of sentences that fit with your normal communications. Practice and learn it!

You will see that many of the techniques for dealing with these Toxic People are not exclusive to a single type.

What to Say

Reduce the Steamroller's impact by considering some of this language:

> "It seems we've reached a dead end here. Let me think over your ideas."

> "Kim, as I was saying, I have a solution for this problem!"

> "That is very true and is definitely a first step. I'd like your ideas on additional steps."

> "You may be right. Help me understand where you are coming from."

> "As professionals, I know this is something we can resolve. Wouldn't you agree?"

Behaviors to Avoid

With Steamrollers, you must learn not to take their jabs and aggression personally. This is difficult if your feeling of self-worth is below par. Never put yourself down, because one goal of the Steamroller is to feel better at your expense. Stop hiding from them and avoiding them. They will hunt you down and make you pay—in public! In addition, don't act hurt or be too vulnerable. They will eat you alive. Remember that behaviors fail; you don't!

Take II: How It Should Sound

Late as usual! Jerry huffed into the meeting, dramatically pulled out the large leather chair, and spread his papers over his allotted space at the conference table. After taking a quick glance at the agenda he had approved, he loudly said, "Morgan, I've already told you not to distribute the agenda before I arrive. Do I need to remind you again? Or perhaps I should get you, my assistant, a keeper."

Morgan replied, "When we all agreed in the last meeting to have ground rules, it included your point of having an agenda that you approve ahead of time. You signed off yesterday on this agenda. I know how busy you are!"

She continued, "Also, you agreed when we set the ground rules to begin and end on time no matter who was missing. So, we were just following your ground rules. It is working well and saving everyone time so we can all be more productive." She turned to the group and said, "Isn't that right?" Everyone nodded, and verbal affirmations filled the room.

"We have a point person who will bring you up to date on what we have already discussed," Morgan added. "Jake, why don't you and Jerry take five minutes to catch up? The rest of us will take a quick biological break. Great. See you all in five minutes. Thank you, Jerry." Smiling confidently, she picked up her coffee cup and headed for a refill. She knew it had gone well, and she was proud that she had not wavered.

CHAPTER 4

The Zipper Lip

❙ ❙ ❙

Take I: How They Sound

Sally was at it again—not contributing to the team brainstorming meeting. Jim, the team leader, was tired of Sally's lack of participation and concerned because she didn't seem to be carrying her weight. The entire company was working with limited resources, including minimal staffing numbers, so they needed every single member of the team to commit, communicate, and share their expertise. Sally had become deadweight and a real pain to the team members who counted on her.

Names Will Never Hurt Me

People like Sally are also known as clams, tight lips, cautious thinkers, madly mysterious individuals, or verbal anorexics. They fail to share their knowledge, opinions, or ideas. By failing to contribute, they become a drag on any work group.

What to Look For

Rarely does the Zipper Lip give good eye contact. Their stance is one of cocooning, including closed body language and typically poor posture. They use escape behavior—"I don't know" is their way to avoid involvement. Single-word responses like "yes" or "no," or just a grunt, are typical of the way they choose to communicate. Their total silence and the little facial animation they show in reaction to others' comments or questions usually heighten the level of frustration for everyone who has to work with them. The difficulty arises because others have no idea what they are thinking. Do they fear making a mistake? Are they trying to be mysterious on purpose to create a sense of power? Does their "don't ask, don't tell" policy stem from previous bad experiences with political power plays? Who knows? And most people stop caring!

The fact is, few people care about the reasons for the behavior. They are more upset because the Zipper Lip may as well be absent if he or she just clams up instead of sharing ideas or plans. Mystery may be intriguing in the movies, but it makes collaboration and shared decision making tedious rather than productive.

The Message the Zipper Lip Sends

Most co-workers rightfully interpret the Zipper Lip's message as a warning against any request or confrontation. The result is that people stop trying to communicate with them. For Zipper Lips, their silence gives them a feeling of control. You learn to leave them alone because you don't have the skill to deal with the uncomfortable silence. Another observation you may have made is that if you push Zipper Lips too far and keep asking them to share their ideas, they may blow up. It's a great way for them to keep people at arm's length. Sometimes, the message is a subtle put-down. Their body language and lack of response can signal, "If you don't know, I can't help you," or "That's really not something worth discussing."

The Payoff for the Zipper Lip's Toxic Behavior

Zipper Lips have little, if any, feeling of personal accountability for the outcome of team. Lack of participation becomes their standard approach. They figure if they say nothing, no one can blame them. If there is a problem, a missed deadline, or an unhappy client, they are not responsible and therefore don't have to be part of the solution. They complete whatever task they are assigned: no more and no less. Their pattern of little or no participation keeps them safe — at least in their eyes. Often they don't actually do anything wrong; they're just not contributing much. They believe knowledge is power and don't understand that *sharing* their knowledge is the real power.

Survival Tactics

You must not ignore the Zipper Lip's silence. Your initial communication with this team member should be conducted in private. Say that you need their help. If fear is a factor in their choice of communication style, then a safe environment must be created or they will pull even further into their cocoon. You also should determine something that they could contribute and get their permission to share it with the group. This can help create the safe environment. Be patient, because you may have to try this approach several times. It may also be worthwhile to have others from the team make the same plea to the Zipper Lip to support your request.

Creating communication ground rules with the group, team, or individual is critical for dealing with all difficult behavior types, but especially so with the Zipper Lip. Allow the entire group to identify critical items. Don't create the list yourself, because it will appear to the group to be contrived and they will not buy in. The final list should look something like this:

General Communication Ground Rules
■ Be accepting of others' opinions and keep an open mind.
■ Be truthful and respectful.
■ Use open body language.
■ Always approach with positive intent.
■ Listen; turn off your own self-talk.
■ Respectfully question ideas you do not understand.

Meeting Ground Rules
■ Have an agenda.
■ Stick to the agenda.

▌ Begin and end on time.

▌ Rotate facilitators.

▌ Everyone participates (round-robin style and no one can pass).

▌ Allow one conversation at a time.

▌ Keep comments brief.

▌ Do not restate what has already been said.

Your group will have some different items listed. Even if you are not the meeting facilitator, team leader, or manager, you should recommend creating ground rules. The benefit to the group is to save time and make gatherings more productive. I know that half the time you spend in meetings is wasted! So, stop it. Take control, and get as much out of each meeting as possible — especially with the Zipper Lip!

What to Say

Remember that silence is their payoff. Train yourself to identify them in your own mind as Zipper Lips and then ask questions that start with *what, why, when, where,* and *how.* This will help them process your request and make it easier for them to share their thoughts:

"*What* questions do you have?"

"Could you explain *why* we need to use the Widget software instead of the Acme software?

"*When* do you think the deadline should be?"

"*Where* else can we look for resources to help us?"

"*How* much budget do you think this project needs?"

Study the following sentences and make them part of your approach when dealing with a Zipper Lip:

"It seems like you're giving this some thought. Tell me two things that are coming to mind."

"I expected you to have responded by now and you haven't, so I'll just wait."

"I need to know how you feel about this."

Behaviors to Avoid

Don't let Zipper Lips think they are getting away with being quiet. Train yourself to call them on their behavior—just be tactful and timely. Don't validate their lack of communication by giving them the cold shoulder. This just backs them further into their shells. Don't blame yourself. This is about *their* choices about how to gain control or feel secure. Criticism will just make them more silent and withholding.

Take II: How It Should Sound

Sally was at it again—not contributing to the team brainstorming meeting. Jim, the team leader, was tired of Sally's lack of participation and concerned because she didn't seem to be carrying her weight. The entire company was working with limited resources, including minimal staffing numbers, so they needed every single member of the team to commit, communicate, and share their expertise. Sally had become dead weight and a real pain to the team members who counted on her.

Wisely, the team had set ground rules early and agreed that if there were any members not showing the proper behaviors, anyone could approach the issue, either privately or within the group, to address the problem. Jim set up a coffee meeting with her. He was straightforward and said, "Sally, I'm concerned about your lack of enthusiasm and input with the team. As you know, we as a team set ground rules on how we would interact and communicate. As the spokesperson for the group, I'd like to hear what needs to happen to get you to participate." Sally said nothing, and Jim had to repeat his request. Still nothing. He then reminded her of the specific ground rules they had set.

Staying calm, Jim continued, "I know you are great at finding the pieces of the plan that we typically overlook. Personally, I need your help and would like to hear your suggestions." Timidly, Sally offered, "Well, there was one thing. . . ." and the conversation was under way. Jim asked her approval for him to share this tidbit with the group. In the next meeting, Sally saw the positive response Jim received. As she felt more comfortable, she began to contribute to the meetings.

If you are saying to yourself right now, "That will never work in my situation!," you are right. You have trained yourself to buy into the Zipper Lip's poor behavior and lack of accountability. Try a different approach. You will be amazed how well it works.

CHAPTER 5

The Backstabber

▌ ▌ ▌

Take I: How They Sound

Carol had worked hard to build a wonderful relationship with the company president, Jeffery. Lynn was hired in a similar capacity and immediately started a campaign to bring down Carol and undermine Jeffery's confidence in her. She told him some untrue stories about Carol criticizing his leadership capabilities. The fables were believable, and Carol heard through the grapevine that there was a chance she would be fired and Lynn would take her position.

Names Will Never Hurt Me

You may have heard Backstabbers like Lynn being referred to as psychopaths or snakes in suits. Interestingly, as many as one out of every 30 people in high-performing business situations has been identified as a Backstabber. This rate is several times higher than that of the general population. Are you surprised? These people have little conscience or ability to develop one. Their only goals seem to be power and personal gain. Maybe you've seen Backstabbers ruin other people's careers. Maybe you've been hurt by one yourself.

What to Look For

Backstabbers are gossips, and not only are they an integral part of the grapevine, they usually are the vineyard manager! Backstabbers spread damaging rumors and try to break down existing friendships. Taking credit for others' work and finding reasons to blame other people whenever anything goes wrong are typical behaviors for them.

Their cleverness includes quickly determining other people's limitations and taking advantage of their weaknesses. Attacking from behind and not directly, they cleverly stab with words and wound with put-downs, and then they have the gall to hide and pretend they have done nothing wrong. Interestingly, they are good at building alliances and will try ganging up before attacking.

> *Backstabber Sam found out that Sara was very shy and nervous, especially when presenting. Building a relationship with her was critical for his gain. He set up a team meeting and nominated Sara to present to the senior leadership group, encouraging the rest of the team to back him up in this decision. At the last minute, Sam changed the PowerPoint presentation and focus of the meeting, sending Sara into a spin.*

She failed miserably, and Sam jumped in and rescued the situation, making himself look like a hero to the leadership group.

The Message the Backstabber Sends

You have already figured out that if you mess with Backstabbers they will get you later. Messages they send include:

"Be careful what you say about me, or I'll say something that will embarrass you in front of others."

"There is nothing you can do to stop me; I'm more clever than you are."

Sometimes Backstabbers will even send another kind of message, such as, "I'm only trying to be helpful. Maybe you don't see the weakness in yourself. It's lucky for you I'm honest. Listen to my feedback if you want to succeed."

Survival Tactics

You need to try to build a positive relationship with Backstabbers and anyone they have enlisted. The more your coworkers like you, the less they will side with them. *Never* say anything negative about the Backstabbers. If they find out, they will turn *you* into the troublemaker.

If a Backstabber tells you that someone else in the office doesn't like you or has it in for you, go to the person directly and ask if it's true. The Backstabber has probably told the other person a similar story about you. These lies can be exposed when there is good communication in your workplace. And yes, it is your job to start the process of clarification. Don't wait for it to improve on its own.

Keep careful records if you truly believe the Backstabber is trying to ruin your career. You need dates, times, information, interactions, and other data. Use a daily planner or calendar. You can then substantiate what has actually happened. When you can, indicate witnesses and include their approval.

If you are told by the Backstabber's boss to do something that you do not think is appropriate, e-mail them as to your understanding of the request. Print a copy and keep an electronic copy with your calendar. You then have proof of what happened, and the blame cannot be placed on you.

If you are going to talk directly to the Backstabber, write down precisely what you will say. Focus on keeping ownership and personal accountability by emphasizing what you need. Remember to use "I" language. "You" language is interpreted by Backstabbers as a real threat and will only make them more aggressive. Be ready for them to try to frustrate and confuse you.

Saying, "I want to make sure we have come to a common understanding on the expected outcomes of this project. I don't think I was as clear as I need to be" will be far more productive than pointing the verbal finger with "you" language. Remember, the Backstabber is clever so you must use language that is not confrontational.

Use direct eye contact without staring; blink every eight to nine seconds to make your gaze look natural and interested. No fluttering or blinking too much! These are signs of weakness, nervousness, and fear. Try to stand when you speak with them and keep one foot slightly in front of the other. This helps you project a confident and competent image and allows you move with energy (not threat) toward your Backstabber. Above all, stay pleasant and focus on the positive intent of the interaction.

What to Say

Being prepared with exactly what you want to say allows you to stay on track and achieve the outcomes you want.

> "That did sound like you were serious. Do the rest of you feel that way? Is this becoming a problem?"

> "I understand that you're unhappy with the plan. Your feedback is important. I want to hear what you think."

Behaviors to Avoid

Never overlook the damage Backstabbers can do. Don't laugh at them or shrug off their behavior. If you do, it just reinforces their control and their negative behavior. They won't change, because this Backstabber behavior has worked for them in the past.

Take II: How It Should Sound

Carol had worked hard to build a wonderful relationship with the company president, Jeffery. Lynn was hired in a similar capacity and immediately started a campaign to bring down Carol and undermine

Jeffery's confidence in her. She told him some untrue stories about Carol criticizing his leadership capabilities. The fables were believable, and Carol heard through the grapevine that there was a chance she would be fired and Lynn would take her position.

Carol began her own campaign by building a positive relationship with Lynn, the same way she had with Jeffery. She was positive and optimistic, although that became more difficult as she learned how Lynn operated. Carol was careful to take on projects orchestrated by Lynn and made sure she had written instructions and completely understood the expected outcomes.

When Carol had questions about one of Lynn's delegated projects, she brought up the issues at her regular coffee meeting with Jeffery. She didn't approach the situation as a tell-all but rather as an "I need your advice and comments" opportunity. Jeffery was surprised at the work and asked who had initiated the venture. Carol told him the project was Lynn's idea, and recommended a meeting with the three of them to strategize. Time-consuming as it was, the meeting led her to the conclusion that she anticipated. Carol called Lynn's bluff and, as a result, wound up as the one managing the department. Lynn was subsequently fired for poorly using the company resources.

CHAPTER 6

The Know-It-All

■ ■ ■

Take I: How They Sound

Frank was disgusted with the meeting agenda, the client, and his col-
leagues. Who were the simpletons who continued to question his skill?
Didn't they recognize the extent of his expertise? Polly approached
Frank about a problem they were having with the client in hopes of set-
ting a plan before the client's arrival. Frank immediately snapped, "I
don't know who is more stupid—you or the client!" When the meeting
started, Frank's negative attitude and arrogance filled the air. The
client was tired of Frank's smart-alecky approach and asked that he be
removed from the project. This would be a real problem, because Frank
did have excellent knowledge and understood what was needed to sat-
isfy the client.

Names Will Never Hurt Me

The Know-It-All pattern of behavior is all too familiar, especially among technical experts, doctors, engineers, attorneys, and other highly skilled and educated people. It is not exclusive to these people, though, and many other professions share the tendency as well. These people are also called content experts, authorities, and the "always right."

Real experts can be an asset, but beware of the pseudo Know-It-All. They are dangerous because they speak well and make you believe what they are saying, when in fact they could be leading you and your plans astray. Making up details in an effort to look good is their usual method of operation.

What to Look For

Ask a Know-It-All a simple question, and you'll get a response something like, "How *dare* you question me or my judgment!" If you didn't know before, this type of response will confirm that a Know-It-All has just been identified.

Or consider a routine business situation where you make a suggestion that you know is sound and in response you get back excuses about why it shouldn't be done that way, why that is not true, why the person you're talking with has a better plan, yada yada yada. Eventually, you give up trying to work with them. Their message of "I'm just like you but smarter" gets old.

The core of the Know-It-All behavior is arrogance. Arrogance gives the Know-It-All a defense against vulnerability and insecurity, often learned in childhood when parents constantly criticized him or her for not being good enough. Think about what you were told while you were growing up. If your best efforts were put down, or every minor flaw was pointed out as an example of your mediocrity, learning how to protect yourself would come easily.

I can remember times when I'd study my guts out and manage to get a hard-won grade of B, only to have my mom say, "Well, if that's the best you can do, that's all I can expect."

Not exactly motivating, right? Well, some people can brush that off, but to the Know-It-All, the best defense is a good offense, as the saying goes. They use their experience as a sledgehammer to make it difficult for others to challenge or question their ability. What a shame they never learned about the power and impact of collaborative problem solving or decision making. Nevertheless, your job isn't to reform them; it's to manage your own response to people who want to push your buttons.

Yes, I've been a Know-It-All myself, and I can tell you, it's not pretty. In the past, I was so afraid of being seen as incompetent that I would immediately throw up a defensive shield against any possible attack. This defense protected me for a while, but everyone else saw right through it. How about you? Are you mature enough to realize this behavior in yourself or others? Do you know what to do?

I learned that when you play the Know-It-All, you lose credibility and respect—the very thing you fear most. What happens then? People refuse to deal with a Know-It-All when possible. When the Know-It-Alls can't be completely avoided, they aren't trusted. Their puffed-up half-truths and fabrications destroy credibility, and others don't believe them or rely on their judgment. In extreme cases, the question of just how competent they really are emerges, and their inability to inspire others to work with them may even be cause for dismissal.

Know-It-Alls are easy to identify because they present their opinions very aggressively. Their tone is usually condescending and their body language implies superiority. Because of their closed thinking, there is little or no room for opposing ideas or new approaches. Blaming others if their ideas backfire validates the essential negativity of their thinking, but the real telltale behavior is their steadfast refusal to consider any but their own views.

The Payoff for the Know-It-All's Toxic Behavior

Know-It-Alls will also make fun of others to deflect criticism. Their unspoken messages often convey not-so-subtle points such as, "You're too stupid to challenge me" or "Be careful or I won't tell you what you need to know and you'll fail." Know-It-Alls may not actually say these things aloud, but the implied message is often painfully emphasized.

Know-It-Alls really believe that there is nothing you can do but accept their wisdom because they are more clever than you. Having you feel lucky to be sharing their wisdom helps you spot the weakness in yourself; at least so they believe!

The shame of the myth of the Know-It-All is that they actually begin to believe they are superior, and this only serves to boost their arrogance. Employers in today's environment will not tolerate this kind of behavior and often choose to "free up the future" of the Know-It-All.

Sometimes it is good to be a Know-It-All. Once when I was nine years old, I was fishing with my dad and my cousin Georgie in Wisconsin.

Georgie was a year younger. His fishing capabilities, especially casting with a live worm on the hook, left much to be desired. On one of his swings with the pole, his hook caught me in the back. My yelp could be heard around the world. All I could think of was a rusty hook and a half-dead worm in my back. Mr. Know-It-All, my father, told me to take a deep breath and not worry. He said that because this kind of accident was more common than I would think, he had asked the doctor for a special serum to use to deal with puncture wounds. After he dug down deep in his tackle box, I could hear the lid pop off a container and then felt the cool, soothing miracle liquid on my back. No infection resulted and, as you can tell, I did not die of some dreaded worm or hook disease.

Twenty-five years later, my dad and I were sitting on a bench on the pier of our Wisconsin lake house. He said coyly, "I have a confession to make. The magic serum I used all those years ago was really just 3-in-One oil. There was no magic serum and no doctor's prescription, but I knew if you believed me and what I was doing, you would be okay." And he was right. Sometimes having a Know-It-All around can be a good thing!

Survival Tactics

Keep Know-It-Alls at bay by asking them to take notes on any discrepancies (and not to verbalize them) as plans or ideas are presented. Ask them to record what they liked best and what can be changed for next time.

- Learn as much as you can from them by asking great questions.
- Ask them for more detail that is specific.
- Appoint them the expert in selected segments of a meeting, project, and so on.

One of the approaches to get along with self-centered coworkers is to butter them up. If you really need to work with them, compliment them into not being so difficult and toxic. Work on getting them to be the center of attention, because they tend to be below-average performers. Given a chance to show off, they may do more than their share of the work. In addition, a lack of self-confidence can be the cornerstone that has pushed this Toxic Person into this Know-It-All behavior. So, the compliment tactic works for yet another reason.

Here is the hard part. You have to keep a sense of humor; otherwise you will have a tendency to just take them out, get the duct tape, and decontaminate them! Know-It-Alls can be a pain, but if you keep a cheerful outlook they can actually become entertaining!

What to Say

Stop being at a loss for words with the Know-It-All. Learn the following responses until they become automatic so you can manage the situation and get the outcome you want.

> "You've presented some strong arguments for additional resources on this project. Now what would happen if . . . ?"
>
> "That sounded like a put-down. Is that what you meant it to be?"
>
> "If I heard you correctly, the major points are . . ."
>
> "Al, you're the expert in this case. Help me understand . . ."

Behaviors to Avoid

Do not try to counter the expertise of someone who has been a Know-It-All for a long time; you'll only set yourself up for disappointment if you try to challenge them. Remember not to sound unprepared or unsure. This behavior is a tip-off to them to attack you at your weakness. In addition, do not embarrass them. They will take their revenge, most likely at a time of greatest damage and/or embarrassment to you.

Caution: Beware of fake Know-It-Alls. They just make up stuff and can be a real problem because they come across as believable and knowledgeable! Call them on their behavior and information immediately and ask them for data to back up their claims.

True Story: Can You Relate?

My company had just landed a huge hospital account that was definitely going to improve our bottom line. The sales representative, John, really pulled a coup for our team. He swaggered around and gloated, making sure everyone knew how much he understood the client and its needs. With the paperwork completed, the administrators began working to place all the print advertising as promised. The guarantees John had made to the client started to unfold.

John was seasoned and knew the parameters of our capabilities, but he had also wanted to wow the client. There was no way our software and database could support half of the promises he had made to the customer. John defended his proposal by stating that he had "checked with the powers that be, and they said the programs were being updated to accommodate these new requests."

John's boss, Ann, brought him in for a meeting with the information technology (IT) manager, who confirmed that the company's current software could not manage the new hospital account as described by John. Included in their conversation was the confirmation that the system was being worked on, but nothing to meet this client's requests and needs would be available for several years. John stated that he knew if he brought in the client, the company would Band-Aid the current system in order to add that kind of revenue. John had used this argument several times in the past and had already been put on notice that it was unacceptable. Promising without being able to deliver got him on the fast track, all right—the one out the door. The Know-It-All lost his job because he really didn't know it all!

Take II: How It Should Sound

Frank was disgusted with the meeting agenda, the client, and his colleagues. Who were the simpletons who continued to question his skill? Didn't they recognize the extent of his expertise? Polly approached Frank about a problem they were having with the client in hopes of setting a plan before the client's arrival. Frank immediately snapped, "I don't know who is more stupid—you or the client!" When the meeting started, Frank's negative attitude and arrogance filled the air. The client was tired of Frank's smart-alecky approach and asked that he be removed from the project. This would be a real problem, because Frank did have excellent knowledge and understood what was needed to satisfy the client.

Before the client had a chance to do anything, Polly chimed in and said, "I know how important it is for you to have an expert on this account. We developed a new policy that there is always a second expert in the wings for all of our clients. I have been shadowing Frank

*and understand most of the issues that need to be addressed." The cus-
tomer was a bit surprised, but pleased, and offered, "I can fill you in on
the other details, and we can move forward." Polly then said, "Frank, I
know you don't mind, because you are really overloaded with work. We
will talk about this later." Frank was put on notice for his poor choice
of words in front of the client and was later fired.*

Decontaminating Toxic People is all about leadership, setting
rules, having consequences for inappropriate behavior, and taking
care of problems as quickly as possible. Don't let the Know-It-All
get you down. Use these skills to do away with the annoying behaviors of the Know-It-All.

CHAPTER 7

The Needy Weenie

▌ ▌ ▌

Take I: How They Sound

Margaret was a high-maintenance team member, but her demands were presented in the form of questions and requests for help. She said yes too much and would wind up being overwhelmed. She committed to more than she could possibly handle, so deadlines were often missed. Her strong need to be involved and to be accepted by everyone was the root of her problem. In meetings, her questions were endless and she was always putting herself down, just waiting for others to build her up. She would restate every point, no matter how simple, in detail. The reason was to support her need for reassurance from other people.

In addition, she had a lot of energy—for all the wrong things. She seemed to focus on everything except what was truly important. In planning the celebration after the completion of a project, for example,

Margaret's agonizing caused the team to spend 20 minutes deciding whether to have a potluck or bring in pizza. Long after heads began to nod, she continued wasting time and spinning her wheels on a decision no one cared about. Something had to be done. Everyone was ready to hang her at high noon!

Names Will Never Hurt Me

People like Margaret are also called agonizers, worrywarts, wimps, vacillators, anxious Annies, and martyrs. They will drive you nuts and make you crazy with their neediness. Their coming back to you repeatedly for validation and help makes you feel like you have a bad rash that just won't go away!

What to Look For

Needy Weenies hate making choices because everything sounds good to them. They are very agreeable and have a strong need to be liked. They often say yes to requests for time and assistance, but they cannot execute because they simply take on more than any one person could do.

Identify a Needy Weenie by listening for words that stall. When you hear "I'll get back with you" or "That sounds good to me; let me think about it," beware! The most difficult part about dealing with these folks is that they are really nice because of their strong need to be liked. In addition, they are very sensitive and will take *everything* personally. The very toxic Needy Weenie seems agreeable on the surface, but there is no consistency when things go bad later. When confronted with a failure to produce, they will hide behind statements like, "Oh that's not really what I meant" or "I said I'd think about it, but I never got back to you so I thought you'd find someone else." The worst part for a business is they miss deadlines or leave teammates hanging!

The Message the Needy Weenie Sends

You can be hooked into being nice to Needy Weenies because they have been nice to you. You feel you owe it to them to be pleasant. Pressuring them only means that they may not make any decision at all. When they say yes they mean maybe. You know they will do anything to get you to like them. You also know they'll want to make you feel guilty if you do anything that's even remotely critical of them.

The Payoff for the Needy Weenie's Toxic Behavior

You need to remember the payoffs for the Needy Weenie. They take few risks, have no accountability for results, and therefore feel no need to change. Others like them, at least at first, because Needy Weenies agree to everything and anything.

William had been with the company for more than 20 years. He was running a sales organization that had never made money within the larger conglomerate despite being in an industry where the competition had an average 65 percent profit margin. When questioned by

61

the president, William would divert the conversation and eventually wind up discussing how to schedule a game of golf on the president's calendar! Early in his career, he had turned into one of the good old boys. Staff and clients loved William because he was so accommodating. He wowed them with lavish parties and assured everyone that their concerns were "right on the top of my list."

Problems arose when the industry began changing fast. Although William promised the department that "Things will get back to normal and we just need to sit tight," it didn't take long for clients, colleagues, and management to discover that his claims were built on shaky ground. His need to be liked led him to overpromise and underdeliver. Before long, clients left for more reliable supply sources, and eventually the sales group was sold.

Despite these negative results, the leaders of the company kept William on—he was "too nice to let go," as one executive said.

This is an example of what happens when leadership is weak and needs to surround itself with needy individuals who will flatter and praise. It would be sad if situations like this were rare, but from my conversations with employees at every level, it continues to happen more often than one might think.

Survival Tactics

William's boss should have made time to clarify the job description and the results expected. Emphasizing the sales orientation of the group, numbers, facts, and results should have been the focus of William's performance reviews. People like William need to be told the rewards of meeting expectations in specific detail. Then William should be asked, "What should the consequences be if these outcomes are not met?"

I have found that this technique works well because people are always much harder on themselves than you ever will be. Often they will say, "I should be fired!" Then you say, "Let's get that in writing." You then document all the reasons for letting them go if they are not doing their job. By the way, this works for many other types, but it is especially effective with the Needy Weenie.

Other tactics that work include reassuring them and their thought processes. Remember, Needy Weenies want to be liked. Language that works well sounds something like this: "I'm glad you basically agree with my proposal. Every proposal has its weak points. What parts could be improved?"

Help them make tough decisions by having them use a pro/con approach to narrow their choices. You might say, "Let's make a list of pros and cons to help clarify this." This is a great approach if there is a stalemate in a project and you can't get them to make a decision or commit to the process. If you want to meet your deadlines and keep the team functioning, you'd better have the tools to deal with Needy Weenies.

Don't feel helpless with these people. Learn to dig deep with them, and keep asking open-ended questions. Always include the question, "Is there anything else?" because there probably is a deeper problem. Help them analyze their thinking and identify the barriers that block progress.

What to Say

Watch overcommitment with Needy Weenies—theirs as well as yours. They love saying yes. Be sure you confirm exactly who will be doing what and according to what time line. When talking with them, the phrase "Another point that popped into my mind was . . ." can be very helpful. It sounds spontaneous and low-key and allows you to provide an easy way for them to avoid taking on one more thing that may end up slipping through the cracks. Normally, I would *never* use that kind of language, but I will with the Needy Weenie because it works.

When you do find that they have overcommitted, approach them calmly and outline the issues/problems. Your goal is to help them get back on track or do damage control before an entire project comes to a screeching halt. Ask them about their progress and follow up with, "What do you want me to do?" or "What kind of help can I provide?" Your job isn't to criticize or try to convince them to change their ways. Your goal is to get the job done — gracefully and successfully.

If you are the manager, this is an excellent opportunity to help an employee grow and develop. Learning to use the right approach and words with a Needy Weenie on a consistent basis can give them the support to move them from this toxic behavior.

Don't just try the approach once or twice and think it will work, because it won't. This is why many fail at managing Needy Weenies. Overlearn each strategy and keep it polished and ready to use at a moment's notice. Craft specific words that are comfortable for you.

Behaviors to Avoid

Try to avoid feeding the Needy Weenies' tendency to agonize by agreeing at any level. I can promise you they will become more needy because you have become a sucker for their neediness. This is hard because they are nice and you don't want to make matters worse! Just remember that behavior that is recognized will be repeated.

> *Samantha was always kind and helpful. The staff started using her desk as the office supply depot—instead of going to the supply room, they would just take what was needed off her desk. Samantha never said a word, and actually encouraged people to take a pen here or a pad of paper there.*
>
> *One day Margo walked over and casually picked up a stapler from Samantha's desk. For Samantha, this was the straw that broke the camel's back! She threw her chair back, jumped up, and shouted, "Why can't anyone leave my stuff alone? I can't believe it! Everyone takes my property, and I'm tired of it!" She slammed the desk drawer and ran to the bathroom crying.*

Beware of explosive Needy Weenies! These are the quiet, seemingly calm people who are always out-of-their-way nice. Then all of a sudden, without warning, something sets them off. Before you know it, an emotional volcano erupts. As survivors of volcanoes can tell you, the cleanup isn't fun, and the consequences far outweigh the Needy Weenies' niceness before the eruption.

I remember when we needed to hire an administrative assistant. An extensive applicant list was narrowed down to a select few who were interviewed by phone and then carefully in person (we had a whole system in place). We hired someone who seemed to have a great ability to function at high energy. We made sure our new hire, who had two hearing aids, could use the phone and perform job duties. She had some problems hearing the hallway pager, but that was not critical. We discussed her needs and ours to make sure she had everything she needed to handle the job successfully.

Training ensued, but by the fourth day we knew it was a bad call. Our applicant was very slow and had more difficulty learning computer software and skills than earlier testing had suggested. She had trouble grasping and retaining lessons. We had made sure she could hear the presentations, so that wasn't it. It soon became apparent she had a learning disability that had not shown up in the application process. She was so sweet and seemed agreeable to everything!

Trying to be straightforward but also supportive, I brought her in and mentioned my concerns about her pace of learning. I spoke very carefully and within a context of what we could do together to address her needs. She responded with anger, threatening, at high volume, to sue for Americans with Disabilities Act (ADA) discrimination. This floored me, since we were going out of our way to accommodate her and help her succeed in her job. Her emotions and reactions had flipped from one extreme to the other.

Our new hire quit before we fired her (which would've happened later that day if she had not left on her own). A few days later, she e-mailed us a very sincere apology for her actions and words, explaining that she was really upset with herself for failing, something she had not done before. I wrote back, telling her she did not fail, that sometimes it takes a few days to find out whether a job is a good match. It would have been easy to ignore the obvious problems because this woman was so eager to be liked and fit in. It was far better in the end for both parties to acknowledge there were problems that couldn't be fixed and move toward a solution.

Needy Weenies come in many forms. I never cease to be amazed at the variations in human nature and the twists and turns our thinking and emotions can take as we deal with one another.

Take II: How It Should Sound

Margaret was a high-maintenance team member, but her demands were presented in the form of questions and requests for help. She said yes too much and would wind up being overwhelmed. She committed to more than she could possibly handle, so deadlines were often missed. Her strong need to be involved and to be accepted by everyone was the root of her problem. In meetings, her questions were endless and she was always putting herself down, just waiting for others to build her up. She would restate every point, no matter how simple, in detail. The reason was to support her need for reassurance from other people.

Margaret's behavior was beginning to weigh on the group, and the worst part was that she felt no accountability to produce. Rob knew there was a way to help Margaret get out of some of these habits. In addition to following the meeting ground rules that the group had previously developed, he asked that a new rule be added: Do not restate what has already been stated.

He also suggested a "three-knock rule," which meant that if anyone was not abiding by the ground rules, any meeting participant could knock on the table three times as a reminder. Rob also decided, even though he wasn't Margaret's boss, that he would suggest that decisions on events such as celebrations be made by a small committee so the entire group's time could be put to better use.

It took a while for the group to get used to the process, but these first steps to managing Needy Weenie behavior made the entire team's work easier!

CHAPTER 8

The Whine and Cheeser

▮▮▮

Take I: How They Sound

Jonathan knew that there must be another reorganization coming because all the bigwigs were in meetings day after day. While talking with Mary, a coworker, he said, "We don't even have the resources we need right now to do the job. Why do they think giving me a new boss every 18 months will make things better? All they really want is to cut costs. What do you think, Mary?"

Mary answered, "I think change is good. It makes us—" Before she could finish, Jonathan cut her off, saying, "Change is awful! All I do is worry about whether the new management will like me and whether they'll like the job I do. I worry they'll bring their favorites with them and get rid of me. I worry about not having enough resources and budgets for all the new projects. They need to leave us alone and just let us do our jobs."

Mary tried to take another approach by changing the topic. "Do you think that Adams project will be done soon?" she asked. With a deep sigh, Jonathan replied, "The Adams project? What a mess! Talk about something that should be changed! We should just dump the entire idea of customer satisfaction—it's just a joke, anyway." Giving up, Mary made a mental note to mention Jonathan's negative perspective during his team input and 360-degree performance reviews. She knew the futility of arguing with him or trying to change his mind. Jonathan, the Whine and Cheeser, had done it again. He had infected the rest of the group with his negativism. Over time, his constant whiny tone and "oh no" attitude brought down even the most positive person.

Names Will Never Hurt Me

You've heard these people referred to as whiners, bad apples, complainers, faultfinders, naysayers, maybe people, and losers. They drain energy out of projects and out of people. Because they have little incentive to improve their lot, the Whine and Cheesers tend to stay on board while their more talented, positive, and motivated colleagues move on.

What to Look For

Chronic complaining has become an epidemic. In some work environments, there are Whine and Cheeser parties about everything, including job duties, supervisors, colleagues, office supplies, the weather, and traffic—nothing is off limits for them. The coffee is too hot; the doughnuts are stale. Fast food isn't fast enough, and restaurants serve the food too quickly and don't let you finish.

These people are terminally upset with almost everything in their lives. They feel disconnected and lonely, and get the attention they crave by complaining. The main problem with their approach is they receive attention, all right, but it's the kind that pushes people away. They don't know how to get positive attention. They have not learned to ask for what they want in a way that makes others receptive.

The team had decided to use an available cabin by the lake for their leadership retreat. Martha was excited about the plans even though she knew there would be some challenges with her wheelchair. Upon arriving, she saw fellow attendees boarding a pontoon boat in preparation for a quick cruise around the lake. No one saw Martha arrive, so the would-be sailors were oblivious of her sitting in her wheelchair on the path toward the cabin. Martha, meanwhile, sat there seething, furious with her teammates. "Didn't they know I wanted to go? How insensitive! I thought they were my friends," she said to herself.

The group returned and eagerly greeted Martha, who, cold and bitter, barely responded to their comments. Finally, one of her colleagues asked what was wrong. Her reply was a classic Whine and Cheeser retort: "If you don't know, I'm not going to tell you!" Mind reading is not a talent most people have. Her teammates were truly puzzled by her attitude. Had she simply admitted she had looked forward to the boat tour, another trip could have been easily arranged. Instead, Martha managed to put a damper on everyone else's spirits without doing a thing to improve her own.

Whine and Cheesers will complain about a beautiful day, a new job, and even a pay raise. They live on the dark side of the moon. Criticizing everything around them is their custom. It is interesting that they often alternate their whiny tone with an accusatory one. They really have no clue how to involve others and get people motivated to go along with their issues. Adding to the problems they cause for themselves and others is their willingness to be equal-opportunity blame spreaders. They take your time complaining about others, then turn around and complain about you to someone else. No wonder people come up with creative ways to avoid these folks. Who wants to spend time with those who specialize in problems rather than solutions?

The Message the Whine and Cheeser Sends

You can probably hear the tone of the Whine and Cheesers' voices when you think of the message they send. Working hard to stay in control and not get angry is your responsibility.

"Don't expect me to do anything to fix problems—I'm helpless."

"To stay on my good side, you must listen to my complaints."

"Don't annoy me, or I may talk about you to other people."

"I'm perfect. Therefore, it is my duty to notice all of the faults around me."

"I'm right, so you had better be sure to listen to me."

Most Whine and Cheesers learned this behavior as children. Maybe they had parents who modeled this behavior. Maybe whining was the only way to get attention. Maybe honesty and feelings were criticized or ignored. Whatever the reason, complaining is a habit, and a self-defeating one at that.

The Payoff for the Whine and Cheeser's Toxic Behavior

Zero responsibility is the name of the game for the Whine and Cheesers. In addition, they annoy others so much that they are ostracized from the group, and that is their goal—to be left alone and have no personal accountability. Frequently, they will not be asked to accept additional work or responsibilities because no one wants to hear their constant complaints and rants.

Survival Tactics

Don't agree with the Whine and Cheeser. Ever. They are famous for interrupting others and cutting them off to add their negative comments. Learn to stop them by saying courteously, "That's not the way I see it. My point of view is . . ." or "I choose to take a more positive perspective, because I have found that gets me better results." Don't pause or hesitate, because that space will give the Whine and Cheeser an opportunity to continue with their negativity.

Another great approach is to ignore their complaints when in public, then corner the Whine and Cheeser privately. In this approach, you should use "I" language and not "you" language. Keeping total responsibility for what you are saying is critical, because the minute you begin pointing the finger with "you" language you will start pushing them even further into pessimism. This may not change them, but you will feel much better! More important, you will have modeled what a proactive message sounds like.

What to Say

Do not let these people suck the life out of you. Memorize a statement that fits with your situation and use it on the Whine and Cheeser and say it repeatedly to them because they probably will not hear it the first few times. This lets them know you are not buying into their misery.

> "Are you looking for some specific solutions to this, or do you just want me to help you look into the problem?"

> "Did you want me to comment or just listen?"

> "Let's take a moment to focus on the good points. What idea appeals to you the most?"

> "From what I've seen, I don't think that is true. Whenever I've gone to her with a problem she's been really open and helpful."

> "The focus so far is _____ . Is there anything else?"

Behaviors to Avoid

At all costs, do not buy into their misery. If you are having a tough day, avoid the Whine and Cheeser.

When they are telling you their story of woe, unfold your arms and push the energy toward them by leaning forward. Stay pleasant and focused on your goals. In addition, try not to embarrass them. This just gives them more ammunition.

Identify if your Toxic Person is a Whine and Cheeser by listening and watching. Do this as quickly as possible and then take action. Don't fall victim to the Whine and Cheeser. That is their goal!

Take II: How It Should Sound

Jonathan knew that there must be another reorganization coming, because all the bigwigs were in meetings day after day. While talking with Mary, a coworker, he said, "We don't even have the resources we need right now to do the job. Why do they think giving me a new boss every 18 months will make things better? All they really want is to cut costs. What do you think, Mary?"

Mary answered, "I think change is good. It makes us—" Before she could finish, Jonathan cut her off, saying, "Change is awful!" Mary jumped right back in and said, "Oh, Jonathan, I wasn't finished with my thought. As I was saying, I think change is good. It makes us find new solutions and keeps the environment dynamic. Personally, I am not going to what-if myself into a frenzy. Let's make a pact right now. I know as two professionals we can do this, Jonathan!" Jonathan frowned, and Mary nudged him. "Oh, come on. Just play along with me, okay?" Mary knew she would have to take this same approach several more times to stop Jonathan's constant negativity. She wished he would go drag someone else down!

Do you want some whine with that cheese?

CHAPTER 9

Planning for Toxic Spills

▮ ▮ ▮

A re you thinking about how hard it will be for you to change? Well, you are right. We are creatures of habit, and change is hard, but not impossible. Because you have continued to read this far, it must mean you are serious about managing Toxic People, decontaminating conflict situations, and resolving dogfights and catfights of the human kind.

In this age of uncertainty, we must challenge the fear we feel when faced with our own change. You can't have a plan of attack if you are fearful of retribution, revenge, paybacks, or bad outcomes. Decontaminating Toxic People is easy when you choose to look at current approaches, evaluate whether they are working, choose to improve, and take a risk.

The root of the problem is that you allow fear to keep you stuck in a downward spiral of negativity, preventing you from moving into action.

> *Bo, the Needy Weenie, was driving you nuts at work. You would see his car in the parking lot and want to turn around and drive home. Taking a different elevator than usual, you'd walk all the way around the office to delay your inevitable encounter with Bo, and then, wham! Just when you thought it was safe, the Needy Weenie would show up. Bo would start in with all the problems of the world. You'd feel like your hair was on fire and want to run away screaming.*

Start to plan your responses today. Don't delay. Don't just think of using one strategy when you plan. Have a variety of approaches. That way, no matter how the conversation changes, you are prepared and ready to neutralize any toxin that is introduced.

> *Jay couldn't sleep at night, because his thoughts kept returning to rumors of reorganization and merger that had been floating around the office for days. What would he do if his job was eliminated? How would he make ends meet and feed his family if he had to take a lesser job? He had so much time invested! What to do? He was angry, anxious, and depressed, and the toxic juices flowed in his body. The stress was affecting his job performance and his personal relationships. He was sick both mentally and physically!*

Every company either has reorganized or is thinking of reorganization. Most employees do not take the time to plan how to market themselves, so they live under the cloud of the "being laid off" fear. Why? Because it takes energy, time, and focus to plan for their next position. Don't get caught in this rut. Take time today and plan for your next job, just in case. Here are six tips to manage the "reorg blues":

1. Get a newspaper, study ads for jobs similar to yours, and determine your fair market wage. You should do this at least every six months anyway! What is your market value?

2. Go online to the many web sites available and look for your current position to verify your salary and benefits. Oh, I know—no one has a job like yours. Just come close!

3. Identify the job of your dreams and determine which companies offer this type of position. Really, think big. If it were a perfect world, what job would you take?

4. Update your resume so it reflects the nuances of today's marketplace. People want to know what you can do for them, not what you've done in the past! Identify what you bring to the party and how you can help the company succeed. Soft skills and hard skills should be included.

5. Find an interesting company? Do your research on its financials, core values, mission, and goals. Can you live with them? Do they match your set of standards or at least come close?

6. Keep sniffing around. Most people will *never* do this, because planning takes time and energy. Don't get lazy. Start this process today.

I challenge you to be ready: If you wind up in a situation that is intolerable because of Toxic People, be ready to bail. Otherwise, *you'll* become the Toxic Person.

I am convinced people become toxic and drag down the rest of the team because they are unhappy. They want everyone around them to feel miserable, too.

Managers don't put into place actions that can be used with these bad apples. They transfer them to someone else's work area and say things like, "They will be just perfect on your team. We just never developed the chemistry." That is probably because the bad apple created a toxic spill, and the manager never learned how to clean it up. Instead of evaluating the person and planning for improvement, managers complete glowing evaluations simply because they don't have the guts to broach the subject. They don't know how to tell Toxic People the truth and put them on an improvement program. Managing fear is very simple. Learn where it comes from and how to deal with it.

In addition, it's not always the manager's place to clean up the toxic spill. It is *everyone's* responsibility to learn how to manage these people. So, stop pointing fingers and making excuses.

Jane was ticked off once again. Maryann had been reassigned to her team. The last time this happened, the results were deplorable. Jane decided to take action. She approached the team members and had them determine "rules of engagement and expectations." She put each of the individuals in charge of keeping within the parameters they had set. When Maryann fell back into her old habits of not doing her job, one of the team members would notice the behavior and approach her. It wasn't a personal approach or attack; the rules of engagement were simply being addressed.

Strategies to Reduce Fear

Successful people apply strategies that lessen the fear of the future and what it can (and probably will) afford them.

SEPARATE CAUTION FROM FEAR

Caution is an intelligent response to a real threat. Fear is an exaggerated response to an imagined or inflated threat. For example, have you ever seen Toxic People explode when they don't get their way? Your fear heightens when you know you are the one who must approach these human volcanoes with information that runs contrary to what they want. The trick is to know you have practiced communication skills, bolstering your confidence for the approaching conversation.

When you feel helpless, remain calm and take an outsider's view to accurately assess the level of true danger. Have an out-of-body experience and look from the outside in; then take reasonable precautions. Example: Your internal language of "What if . . ." can push you into bone-chilling fear. What are you saying to yourself? Are your words instilling fear? Do you feel fearful because your perception of the situation is distorted? Force yourself to proceed with caution.

> *"Here we go again," Vern thought to himself. "The last time I had to address the group, Elizabeth nailed me! What if I screw up again? What if I get kicked off this team? What if I lose my job? What if I can't find a new one? What am I going to do?" Vern stopped himself, knowing he was sending himself into a downward spiral.*

BE OPTIMISTIC

Fear is selfish—yes, selfish, because it turns you inward. When you take responsibility for your outcomes in a positive fashion with your work groups, your friends, and even total strangers, it forces you to turn outward. Example: Michael J. Fox was diagnosed with Parkinson's disease, but rather than surrender to the fear that accompanies the diagnosis of a progressive neurological illness, he used his celebrity stature to become a leader in the efforts to find a cure for Parkinson's. Would you be able to do this? If you question your ability to turn toxic situations into more positive outcomes, you need to improve the belief you have in your talents and skills.

> *Vern continued, "I am in control here. I've got to interrupt this stupid negative thinking. I'm a smart guy and can handle this if I just stay in control and not let my fear take over. I know I can turn this trepidation into energy and be really good at relaying my information to the team!"*

DEVELOP TRUE BELIEF IN YOURSELF

You are the big kahuna. You are as good as it gets. Understand who you have become and strictly live by your core values. Be assertive and always stand up for your rights while not violating the rights of others. Self-awareness and confidence allow a realistic view of the current events and will help you evaluate your fears more objectively.

Practicing decontamination strategies in his personal life reinforced Vern's capability to handle ugly situations. When faced with toxic spills, he knew this was the world's way of testing what he was learning. When the outcomes were not exactly what he planned, he evaluated the situation by asking himself, realistically, what he did well, and always finished up with what he should work on next time to get a better result.

DO SOMETHING

Fear can immobilize you. Forcing yourself to do something—anything—can change the focus and free you from fear. Learn, read, take a class—just do it. Knowing that you have the skill and information to proceed can erase the fear. When soldiers are asked whether they're frightened in battle, they often answer that they're not afraid while the fighting goes on, but they are while waiting for the fighting to begin. The mental process of failure can be terrifying.

Vern knew one of his weak areas was matching body language and energy level. Focusing on something this simple helped him manage toxic spills. He read that a very subtle way to manage anger or a people problem is to match body language and energy using a technique called mirroring. He started training himself to watch the way people enter a room, how they interact in a group setting, their choice of words, and how they solve problems. Mirroring others' behavior gave him the strength and training to evaluate every situation.

REMIND YOURSELF THAT FEAR HOLDS YOU BACK

You are in control, but you will become what you think about. Fear makes you reluctant to approach difficult people, so you remain in negative, toxic environments. You become a victim of circumstance. If you are afraid to explore the world and afraid to live (and I mean fully live), there is a ripple effect that extends to others. When you reveal your fears to your children, you raise kids who are fearful themselves!

> *Vern knew his biggest problem was developing consistency when using his new skills. He would not let fear keep him from developing the uniformity he needed.*

Face Down Fear!

Think about where Vern was coming from and ask yourself if you relate. I don't care how sophisticated and practiced your skills are; there are times when you are fearful. If you don't see this in yourself, you have become one of the six types of Toxic People! Your capability to clean up the toxic spills will be limited.

A fearful mind concocts trepidation all by itself! Remembering past negative outcomes creates the trepidation you feel in a new situation. When this happens, most people either withdraw or get angry with themselves because they don't feel capable. This means your anger is self-induced. Other people and events don't make you angry; it's the way you evaluate and internalize them. You get ticked off because you are out of control. And it's not anyone's fault but yours.

Focus on Resolution

Here is a 10-step plan for dealing with toxic behavior.

1. Identify the Toxic Person's behavior.
   - Review the six types of Toxic People and determine with whom you are dealing. Reread Chapters 3 through 8.
   - What is the incentive for this type of behavior?
   - Do they change from one type to the next? If so, expand your planning to include the different toxic types.
2. Understand the outcome you want with the relationship.
   - Do you need to resolve the issue and move forward with this Toxic Person?
   - Is it better to sever the relationship completely?
   - Should you set up definitive parameters on how the relationship will proceed?
3. Decide how you want to be perceived by the Toxic Person.
   - Do you want this person to respect you as a team member?
   - Are there other people concerned about your relationship, like your leader? What is their desire?
   - Do you even care what the Toxic Person thinks of you? (Don't be cavalier; really think about the importance of this question!)
4. Plan your response to your Toxic Person.
   - List your options using this book and other resources to expand your thinking.
   - Understand the payoff for someone choosing this behavior.

- Be accountable for what you are going to say.
- Have different approaches so you can be flexible as the conversation develops.

5. Practice your approach.
   - What will you say to yourself to stay on target with your plan?
   - How will you check your own anger or anxiety during the approach?
   - If you want to ensure your success, practice by recording yourself.
   - Listen to the recording and decide how *you* would respond to the tone, words, and delivery.

6. Choose the appropriate time and environment.
   - Look at the Toxic Person's energy level at different times of day. Some people are better communicators and more tuned in first thing in the morning than later in the day.
   - Is it better to meet in their office, yours, or a neutral place?
   - Decide how the room should be arranged. My preference is to be on their strong side (i.e., their right side if they are right-handed).
   - If there are windows in the room, where do you want the light source? My preference, being a power junkie, is to have the light at my back, but not too bright.
   - Will you wear power clothes?

7. Follow up with the person if appropriate.
   - If this is someone you need to have a continuing relationship with, decide how and when you will follow up with them after your conversation.

- ▌ Don't hide from Toxic People. This can deepen the problems you have with them.
- ▌ Don't gossip with anyone about your interaction.
- ▌ If appropriate, share the results of your meeting with your leader.
8. Evaluate the meeting by yourself.
    - ▌ Did you achieve the outcome you planned for?
    - ▌ Is your Toxic Person okay with the results?
    - ▌ Did your planning pay off?
    - ▌ What did you do well? You can be proud of yourself, because most people just let toxicity permeate relationships!
9. Determine what you can improve the next time you encounter this kind of Toxic Person.
    - ▌ What did you learn that you can apply next time?
    - ▌ Make a note of your discovery in a journal to build your knowledge.
    - ▌ If the situation with your Toxic Person reaches an approachable point, ask what their initial thought was when you approached and spoke to them.
10. Give yourself a pat on the back!

Congratulations! You deserve it! Continue to refer to this list every time you have to manage a toxic situation, and do this until all the habits become second nature. If you just use these ideas two or three times, they cannot really become ingrained into your head, and you will soon fall back into your old habits. Remember that rehearsal and practice give you the outcomes you want from any toxic spill!

Send a message to Information@MarshaPetrieSue.com if you would like to receive the Planning Worksheet.

Planning Worksheet

1. Identify the Toxic Person's behavior.

_____

_____

_____

_____

_____

_____

2. Understand the outcome you want with the relationship.

_____

_____

_____

_____

_____

_____

3. Decide how you want to be perceived by the person.

    _____

    _____

    _____

    _____

    _____

    _____

4. Plan your response to your Toxic Person.

    _____

    _____

    _____

    _____

    _____

    _____

5. Practice your approach.

    _____

    _____

    _____

    _____

    _____

    _____

(Continued)

Planning Worksheet *(Continued)*

6. Choose the appropriate time and environment.

_____

_____

_____

_____

_____

_____

_____

7. Follow up with the person if appropriate.

_____

_____

_____

_____

_____

_____

_____

8. Evaluate the meeting by yourself.

   _____

   _____

   _____

   _____

   _____

   _____

   _____

9. Determine what you can do to improve the next time you encounter this kind of Toxic Person.

   _____

   _____

   _____

   _____

   _____

   _____

   _____

10. Give yourself a pat on the back!

HOW THE PLANNING WORKSHEET COULD LOOK

SITUATION

Ray works with you, but his only topic of discussion is himself. He is a pain to listen to because the conversation is based on his problems, financial woes, a wife who doesn't understand, his aches and pains, and how no one cares about him.

You have your own personal problems and choose not to discuss them. You have to listen to Ray's issues an hour at a time, and it is driving you crazy. You choose to take action.

Digging through the notes you made while reading this book, you finally locate your planning sheet. (Remember, we will e-mail a copy of the Planning Worksheet for your use if you contact Information@MarshaPetrieSue.com.)

Planning Worksheet

1. Identify the Toxic Person's behavior.

   Because of his constant complaining, Ray is classified as a Whine and Cheeser. He also shows signs of being a Needy Weenie because of his constant need to be listened to. He never takes personal accountability for anything. He is good at following directions but complains the entire time he is working on a project.

---

2. Understand the outcome you want with the relationship.

In a perfect world, Ray would keep his problems to himself and focus on conversations based on work and projects. This would help us build an environment that is productive and way more fun. It would be great if he took personal responsibility for his life. I really think this would make him an enjoyable part of the team.

3. Decide how you want to be perceived by the person.

Since I have to work with Ray, I want to be seen as helping and not pointing fingers or being a manipulator. It would be great if he would see me as helping him to develop better skills to move forward with a more successful relationship with his work group and ultimately his own life.

4. Plan your response to your Toxic Person.

I've decided not to listen to his negativity. I'll be protective of my time and will say, "I really have a lot on my plate right now, and have got to get to my desk" (or whatever it is

(Continued)

Planning Worksheet *(Continued)*

I'm working on). If he is ranting on and on about how awful something is, I'll say, "That's not the way I see it, because I've found that the company does work in my best interest." Or, if his rant is about a person, I'll say something like, "My experience with him/her is completely different. I've got to get back to work right now."

5. Practice your approach.

I vow to myself that I will practice at least three times, without interruption, to become comfortable with my approach and words. I will not fold when I am actually in front of my Toxic Person and will keep my attitude positive. This is really about me building the strength, because I realize I will NEVER change others. I can only change myself, and it is my responsibility to do so.

6. Choose the appropriate time and environment.

I will be aware of when I feel trapped into listening to the endless complaints. I know that I don't have to! Refusing to reward Ray's behavior by becoming his audience will be the basis of my response. My suffering in silence actually gives Ray the belief I am interested.

7. **Follow up with the person if appropriate.**

   I do have to work with Ray, as we are on the same project team. I plan to approach him (rather than always avoiding him) with positive results of something I have done or that happened (even if I have to dig deep for something good!). I will start by saying, "I just have a second, and wanted to let you know the project really took a positive step forward." I will turn quickly and walk away, not waiting for his response.

8. **Evaluate the meeting by yourself.**

   I am very proud of myself for taking the first step to not being sucked into Ray's Whine and Cheeser attitude. The results are not exactly what I wanted. I am closer to having the skill, though, and Ray seems to be leaving me alone a little more. I

   (Continued)

Planning Worksheet *(Continued)*

need to watch my words and approach, because I see that I

can easily fall into some old bad habits.

_____

9. Determine what you can do to improve the next time you encounter this kind of Toxic Person.

I think practicing one or two more times will help with my next

encounter. The words I wanted to use didn't flow the way I had

hoped. I did have some positive results. Checking my own atti-

tude and ensuring I am in the optimistic flow with the out-

come I want will help. Even one of my colleagues said, "Boy,

Ray seems to be leaving you alone a little. What's up?" Yeah! It

is being noticed!!

10. Give yourself a pat on the back!

Just remember practice really does make perfect. Changing approaches and habits is not easy. There is no magic wand, magic fairy dust, or a pill you can take to ease the pain of a Toxic Person. You are the one who must decide to continue the journey to decontaminating Toxic People.

Drama Queen

While getting ready to depart on a flight to Atlanta from Phoenix, the pilot announced that we had an engine leak and the mechanics needed to check it before we took off. The young woman sitting behind me started screaming, "I'm going to die! I don't want to die in an airplane wreck. Oh, my God! What am I going to do?" She proceeded to make phone calls and said the same thing repeatedly. Her friend just sat there looking at her. Drama Queen was more than annoying.

Turning around several times, I tried to reason with her. She just continued her death rant.

The flight attendant walked by, and I stopped her. Standing up, I proceeded to explain that the young woman was too agitated to fly. I said it loudly enough so the distraught young woman could hear me. The attendant asked the young woman whether there was a problem. After hearing the passenger's overly dramatic interpretation of the situation, the attendant gave her two choices: either calm down or get off the plane. Amazingly, the woman calmed down and didn't say another word.

Another Toxic Person had entered the picture, though. While we were waiting, the man in the row to my left was on the phone. He appeared to be speaking with his ex-wife. At least that's what I concluded after hearing him tell her, at a volume that made his message clear to the entire front of the plane, that she was "obviously too dumb to raise an eight-year-old daughter." His choice of language was as off-putting as his tone. Like most Toxic People, he seemed clueless about the effect his words were having on those around him. To call a person like this inconsiderate is like calling the Sahara a sandbox. Unfortunately, the mechanical repairs to the plane had us sitting at the gate for over an hour. And guess who kept up his negative performance until the flight attendant gave him the same two choices she had presented earlier to Drama Queen: calm down or get off the plane. When faced with natural consequences, even this hardened Steamroller changed his behavior.

I share this account because you do not have to tolerate poor behavior and Toxic People. You do not have to be nice. It's difficult to remember the right behavior or communication strategies to use when Toxic People are around. Too often, we become passive; we just take these behaviors at face value. There are times when such acceptance is not enough. Remember the TLC choices discussed earlier. You can take the person as she or he is, leave them or the situation, or work to make changes in your response to them. There are steps you can take to decontaminate Toxic People. What's your plan?

CHAPTER 10

Plotting
Toxic Cleanup

▪ ▪ ▪

Why is it that you can always think of the right thing to say *after* a difficult communication? Because you don't use what you know! VIP (very important plotting: verbiage, intent, and posture) communication tells you to put your mind in gear before opening your mouth.

You know this; you just don't always do it! Understanding how to communicate more effectively is no guarantee that your interactions will automatically improve. Understanding is one thing, whereas achieving a different outcome is another. You have to practice new behaviors over and over to develop a habit. This is just as true for verbal skills as it is for any others.

Habits for VIP Communication

If you want to move into the upper echelon of VIP communicators, you will have to create habits built on what you already know: verbiage, intent, and posture. The fact that you have seen other people manage fights, angry people, and toxic situations proves that these are learnable skills. If you can't deal with Toxic People now, it's not that it can't be done; it's just that you have not yet chosen to learn and polish your skills to get it done.

VERBIAGE

Think of the words that send you into orbit. For me, the phrase "Do you understand?" has a very negative connotation. "Do they think I'm stupid?" is what's going through my head when I hear that phrase. For many people, such comments feel like a verbal slap in the face. Have you had this experience, too? If so, do you ever find yourself doing the same to other people? Why? Eliminate such words today and instead choose to say something like, "I want to make sure I was clear. Can you please play that back in your own words?"

Always give others a reason for listening to you. Choose words that benefit them. VIP conversation should be less about you and more about the other party. Keep in mind that good judgment comes from experience, and much experience comes from bad judgment.

INTENT

Approach toxic situations with positive intent and eliminate the focus of getting them before they get you. Results improve when you anticipate meeting others with a positive intent that focuses on everyone's desired outcomes. Another critical issue is keeping a positive attitude about what you are *capable* of saying. You can do this by filling your mind and mental toolbox with affirmations such as:

> "I have practiced this scenario and understand the words that will ultimately get the best results."

Eliminate all thoughts and visions of a negative outcome when you plan your encounters. Why? Because what you think will influence how you come across to others. People are smart and clever. They can see right through a phony attempt to "meet their needs." In addition, positive intent gives *you* power and control, and isn't that what you ultimately want?

A seeming contradiction to being proactive is the strategy of just letting go. Your intent may be to resolve the situation, but occasionally, in your heart, you know it will never work. You must have a well-developed sense of self-awareness to walk away and know it is the right thing to do. No matter how good your skills or what your intent may be, you will never resolve every situation. Whether it is a boss, a colleague, or a subordinate, there are just some relationships that are not going to work. They should be a small minority—less than 2 percent. And make sure you do not take these irresolvable conversations, situations, or relationships personally. Reaffirm your own thinking process by being sure you *do* evaluate the situation to figure out what you might have done differently, in order to increase your skills for future encounters.

POSTURE

Eliminate emotional posturing and closed body language. Crossed arms, furrowed brow, intense glare, and no smile are physical communication signals indicating that trouble lies ahead. You *know* you shouldn't be doing things like this when working on improving communications. You subconsciously use them because they have become habits. Train yourself to stand with your arms uncrossed, lean forward, push the energy toward the other person, and keep a pleasant, non-threatening look on your face.

Start watching the posturing of others by observing their energy levels. Then when you do have a toxic situation, you are one step ahead. Do they express their thoughts and emphasize their points by using their bodies and gestures? Or are they more reserved physically? They may have a natural drive to conserve energy. These differences are noticeable in group situations, because energetic people gain momentum within a crowd. In contrast, less energetic individuals are drained, causing them to become withdrawn. You can apply this energy observation when approaching Toxic People by matching your energy level to theirs. Remember, your control of the situation comes from watching and waiting.

Watch for animation, or lack of it, in their facial expressions. People who are real thinkers are not facially expressive in general. This means my posturing and body language with them will be less animated. The other side of this is to watch for physical expressions such as pulling a chair closer during a discussion, leaning toward or away from you, or pushing documents to the side. Changes in approach such as attempting to be more diplomatic, becoming highly emotional, or changing the subject provide other cues to respond to.

Posturing is not just physical. How about written communications? Think about how you set up your e-mails. Do you create eye appeal for the reader, or is your message a plethora of words with little structure and rambling requests? Pay attention to what appeals to you and how others arrange elements of their communication.

Put yourself on notice for using negative words. Load your thinking with positive responses and words like "can" and "will," instead of negatives like "can't," "won't," didn't," and "not."

Instead of saying "You make me mad and upset," consider saying, "I am upset when we do not take the time to understand each other's point of view." This restatement is very subtle, and not always easy to remember in the heat of dealing with a Toxic Person. It is, however, the best approach. It's one worth practicing so you have it readily available in your toolbox.

Communicating Results: Quick Reference Chart

Here are 27 ways to say what you mean and get what you want. Record yourself talking and eliminate the phrases that rob you of confidence and good communication outcomes.

USE	ABUSE	WHY
"However . . ." or "And . . ."	"Yes, but . . ."	Avoids discounting what is said.
"You may be right."	"It is not."	Hears other's thoughts.
"Help me understand."	"You are wrong."	Reduces conflict.
"Let's try this."	"That's not practical; it won't work."	Stimulates thinking.
"I need your help."	"Here's why this is good for you."	Aims for cooperation.
"Is everything satisfactory?"	"How can I do better?"	Eliminates the emotions.
"Here's what I can do."	"Here's what I can't do."	Focuses on the positive.
"Let's work together."	"You must do what I say."	Works with others.
"A consideration is . . ."	"You'll have to . . ."	Invites cooperation.
"Please consider . . ."	"I recommend . . ."	Focuses on others first.
"What is the fairest way?"	"Do it my way."	Appeals to equality.
"I understand. I need to look further at . . ."	"I disagree."	Acknowledges ideas.
"I am upset when that happens."	"You make me upset."	Gives power away.
"I choose to make the best of . . ."	"I can't change who I am."	Shows personal accountability.

USE	ABUSE	WHY
"I can manage my available time."	"I don't have time."	Avoids powerless phrase.
"Let's see what we can do."	"Ask someone else."	Be part of the solution.
"I'm getting better at . . ."	"I'm not good at . . ."	Beliefs become reality.
"I planned well."	"I'm lucky."	Creates your own luck.
"What questions do you have?"	"Do you have any questions?"	Eliminates yes, no.
"I hear your point of view."	"I disagree."	Keeps an open mind.
"Sometimes some things . . ."	"Everything always . . ."	Avoids absolutes.
"I'm sorry."	"Don't blame me!"	Admits mistakes.
"Thank you."	"Oh, it was nothing."	Takes credit.
"I want to."	"I hate to."	Focuses on the positive.
"I learned."	"I failed."	Expands skills.
"It's over; that's all."	"What if it gets worse?"	Creates positive results.
"Starting today I will . . ."	"If only I had . . ."	Changes tomorrow.

Please e-mail us at Information@MarshaPetrieSue.com if you would like a copy of the above list.

Take time to understand what will work within communications. Practice being a VIP communicator. Remember that you have control over three things: what you think, what you say, and how you behave. No one controls these but you. Take personal responsibility for dealing with the Toxic People in your life, because if you don't, they will take you down.

Plotting to Manage Toxic Bosses

You do not have to put up with toxic behavior from your superiors. What you *do* have to do is understand how you can avoid becoming a victim of circumstance. This is a really hot topic for me!

It doesn't matter if your boss is any one of the six toxic types or a combination of several types. You have choices on how to handle the problem. Some people are irritating but seldom really harmful to you and your career, whereas others are really out to get you. This is where your personal responsibility lies—to distinguish one from the other.

ILLEGAL OR UNETHICAL BEHAVIOR

You must determine whether your boss's behavior is illegal or unethical. No one else will intercede unless you take action. Don't wait for someone else to figure out what is happening, because they won't. I've found that most people are too afraid to even recognize a problem, much less address it. The reason? They don't respect themselves, their skills, or their capabilities enough to view themselves as having control. How about you?

When your boss displays truly unethical behavior, you must decide whether you can live with just letting it go unaddressed. If you decide to take action, my suggestion is to make sure you consider the working environment before proceeding. If you work in a very small company, there may not be a human resources department. If you have a mentor, he or she would be the best one to consult for a second opinion. If you have not found a mentor, the Equal Employment Opportunity Commission (EEOC) has a

106

web site with suggestions on how to handle your employment problems.

> *Linda enjoyed her boss, colleagues, and job and knew her position was a great fit for her talents and skills. Maggie, her supervisor, called her one day after she had submitted her time and expense report. Linda could hardly believe her ears—Maggie was upset because Linda had not expensed enough for her client lunches. Linda defended her charges by saying, "Well, that was the actual expense. I know it is company policy not to pad the expense account in any way."*
>
> *She was scolded by Maggie, who said, "You're making me look bad. The other manager's expense report is twice yours and he has half the client base! Walk through the graveyard to get names, save some of your personal receipts, and put them on your expense report!" Linda was dumbfounded and needed to think before she could respond. After a long pause, she finally said, "That's an interesting approach," and ended the conversation. She tried to show no emotion or any signs of being upset.*
>
> *An ethical issue was launched, and Linda had to make a decision. The company's human resources department had just distributed new policies that included a statement about "maintaining an ethical working environment," so she decided to approach them. She explained her situation, without using names, to get some idea of the options available to her. She was able to get the answers needed to move forward in a way that maintained her integrity and did indeed contribute to the ethical working environment the company espoused.*

When interviewing for a position, it is your responsibility to determine whether the company environment is principled. Does the mission statement contain language that includes the company's ethical practices? Has the company established a whistle-blower access line? Does it have a human resources department or other resource that helps the employees with workplace issues? It is critical to set yourself up for success. Beware of the Enron syndrome where a job is filled because of greed!

IRRITATING BEHAVIOR

When your boss's behavior is irritating, you must decide to approach him or her. Don't complain or gossip to others—ever. This is your issue, not theirs. You can, however, take a hypothetical situation similar to yours and approach a colleague asking what he or she might do in similar circumstances. You may want to say that a friend of yours working with a different company has the problem. Just be sure to disguise the identifying factors. Coworkers will see right through your approach if it's not done well. They will tell someone else, even if you ask them not to.

> Phyllis had no idea what to do, so she just pretended not to hear. This didn't work for long. Her boss kept on with his inappropriate comments, and the client kept checking Phyllis to see how she would respond. Her facial expressions and nonverbal behaviors suggested she was becoming increasingly annoyed, but she said nothing directly. By saying nothing, she reduced her credibility with the client. She realized she needed to retain the respect of her clients and decided to organize her thoughts about the best way to deal with her boss.
>
> Setting a private meeting with her boss seemed to be the best approach. When the day came, and after much practice, Phyllis met with him, faced him directly, but left her emotions at the door. She simply said, "I would appreciate it if you would refer to me by my name, Phyllis, instead of calling me 'sweetheart' or any other reference."

Her boss responded, "Can't you take a joke? I mean it as a term of endearment!" Phyllis then explained calmly, "I expect that you didn't know how much it bothers me. However you mean it, I want you to refer to me by name, please. You can help me build credibility and respect with my clients by doing this. I know this will help me grow this business."

(By the way, this does happen to men as well; calling someone by a nickname is far too casual for the workplace.)

This will not be resolved in just one conversation. You will have to go back to them a few times for the request to actually sink in. When dealing with sensitive issues, remember: Keep your emotions in check and just stay calm. You must maintain control.

WHAT IS THE COST?

Review the cost of approaching your boss. What might be the fall-out? Is there a chance of getting fired? Transferred? Taunted by peers because your boss has a tendency to talk too much? The best-case scenario is that you resolve the problem and live happily ever after in an otherwise toxic environment. The worst-case scenario? Be sure you know the possibilities as part of your planning.

In addition, and even more important, you have to ask: What is the cost of doing nothing? You have to create an environment that is comfortable for you. Every employee has a different perspective of what constitutes good and enjoyable working conditions. Can you maintain your integrity and self-esteem if you recognize problems but fail to address them?

Do you have a plan set up before you approach your boss so you are ready to launch into the next level of your career? No one manages this for you but you. I am amazed at how many people know this but never take the time to plan for it. How about you? Everything has to be planned for, and you are the planner.

■ ■ ■

Plotting toxic cleanups will allow you to focus on the outcomes you want. It will also stop or reduce disagreeable behavior without insulting the other person. The VIP strategies and ways to manage toxic bosses give you specifics that will help you build your skills, move toward promotion, position you as a leader, and make you a more effective communicator. As companies reinvent themselves, send business overseas, and employ cutbacks, they will keep only those employees who have polished skills. You have to decide whether you want to become one of those employees.

Some readers may have been surprised at my use of the word *plotting* to deal with communication issues. The kind of plotting discussed here is not negative manipulation. It's simply the way you stay in charge and fulfill your career dreams.

CHAPTER 11

Listen Up!

▮ ▮ ▮

Ginger is simply impossible at work. She gets into everyone else's business and finds time to discuss her opinions and personal issues with anyone who will listen. Unfortunately, her boss listens to her and sometimes acts upon her advice. The rest of the team is fed up, ticked off, and ready to quit. Sound familiar? Well, listen up!

You have no clue how to listen. This Toxic Person survival skill is not taught in schools or business. Your parents were supposed to teach you to listen, just as they were supposed to impart sex education when you were in your early teens. In reality, what probably happened was that you learned from their behaviors and modeling more than from their direct instruction the important skill of listening.

There is an excellent possibility that your "listening gland" has atrophied from disuse. Don't think you are alone. The majority of the adult population suffers from the same condition. Much of the conflict you deal with daily originates in poor listening patterns. Toxic People's behavior intensifies because no one listens to them.

I remember being in a restaurant and getting terrible food and service. The server asked, "How was everything?" When I answered honestly and said things were awful, the automatic response was, "Great! You can pay up front whenever you're ready." The server didn't hear a word I said! The good news is I won't have to hear that again from that establishment, because I will never go back. They allowed me to vote with my feet. The sad news is they will probably never understand why their customers continue to desert them.

Busy people can be especially poor listeners. Some have a list of horrible habits and are almost incapable of listening. Are you the kind of person who talks more about yourself in any given conversation? What percent of each encounter do you spend asking questions and listening to the information given by the other person? Studies show that 95 percent of people listen from a self-centered point of view. Their concern is solely about their own outlook, and they use other people to confirm what they already believe to be true. Only 5 percent really pay attention to or focus on the other person. Sad, isn't it?

Ears and Brains

Hearing is a passive physical process. When you hear something, whether a voice or other noise, it just means your ears are working. This is the reason you get upset when someone says, "I hear what you are saying." You subconsciously interpret this as them not listening to you. Do you say "I hear you" to others? I'll bet you do.

Hearing is one of the traditional five senses, and refers to the ability to detect sound. In humans and other vertebrates, hearing is performed primarily by the auditory system: sound is detected by the ear and transduced into nerve impulses that are perceived by the brain.

Herein lies the problem. Your brain has not been trained, nor have your listening skills been practiced, to accept information different from what the brain already knows or expects. In confusion, it just simply doesn't pay attention to the physical sound, and the message isn't processed. Listening is much more than simply hearing.

Here are dictionary definitions:

Hear

1. To perceive or be able to perceive sound.
2. To be informed of something, especially by being told about it.
3. To listen to somebody or something.
4. To understand fully by listening attentively.

Listen

1. To concentrate on hearing somebody or something.
2. To pay attention to something and take it into account.
3. To make an effort to hear something.

Obviously, there is a crossover in meaning. You can simplify this by constantly challenging yourself make a mental note and remind yourself to listen *and* hear, especially when faced with a Toxic Person.

People hear; they just don't listen. Generally, hearing is the intake of sound, not information. Listening uses the brain to access what the words really mean. Hearing can conclude in turbulence, anger, and conflict. Listening, if done properly, results in better outcomes and reduced problems.

Here are five things you typically do when someone else is talking:

1. Think about what you are going to say when it's your turn to talk.
2. Think about something else, like an e-mail you need to send or a phone call to be made.
3. Do your best to take notes on everything the speaker is saying.
4. Evaluate how poorly the speaker is communicating or handling a topic.
5. Wait for silence so you know it's your turn to talk.

"Enough about me. What do you think of me?"

Listening Scoreboard

Do you think you are a good listener? Let's check and see!
Circle the appropriate response and then score yourself.

1. Influencing your listener means you:
   A. Manipulate them to go along with you.
   B. Must both want the same thing.
   C. Get everything you want.
2. Successful influencing leads to:
   A. Short-term solutions.
   B. Long-term problems.
   C. Targets that are adhered to.
3. When you want the other person to listen, make sure you are:
   A. Controlling something controllable.
   B. Standing closer to them.
   C. Letting your emotions show.
4. To get the other person to listen, you should:
   A. Build rapport and trust.
   B. Clearly identify the obstacles.
   C. Point the finger at them.
5. You should keep an open mind and open body language when listening because:
   A. It shows others you respect their thoughts.
   B. Others will open up to you more easily.
   C. This removes communication barriers.

6. When others have finished their story, you:
   A. Paraphrase their message.
   B. Immediately add your opinion and solution.
   C. Be ready to add your rebuttal.
7. Successful people are good influencers because they:
   A. Have specific details to support why they are right.
   B. Ask open-ended questions.
   C. Keep focused on the same problem using the same techniques to get their point across.
8. If you reach a stalemate in attempts to influence the other person, you should:
   A. Drop the subject and terminate the conversation.
   B. Repeat what you have already covered.
   C. Acknowledge and address the stalemate.
9. People who learn how to listen:
   A. Have better encounters.
   B. Encounter fewer occasions that require conflict resolution.
   C. Create an environment of mutual respect, cooperation, and happiness.
10. To improve your listening skills, you should:
    A. Spend more time alone.
    B. Listen to others and their preferences.
    C. Spend more time in groups.

Listening Scoreboard Answers

1. **B.** To succeed, both people must agree on an outcome. Too often, people try to influence others only to achieve their own personal goals. This results in tension in the relationship and in the workplace.

2. **C.** Successful influencing does not take place if an agreement is reached and then later one of the people reneges. Sustain results by agreeing on a common objective initially, keeping open communications, and staying flexible to the other's input.

3. **A.** Don't waste your energy trying to exert influence over areas that you can't control. For example, don't try to change other people—you can only change yourself. Check your body language, tone, and word choice.

4. **A.** People who want others to hear their message develop people skills and know the value of continuing to build rapport and trust. Sarcasm, cynical remarks, negative body language, or bullying tactics will push others away and they will listen less! Building trust on an ongoing basis is one of the most important elements of a successful professional relationship. Use Myers-Briggs Type Indicator results or another assessment as a tool to identify your natural style and strengths. These assessments can make you more sensitive to understanding other styles as well.

5. **A.** Open body language and interested facial expressions show that you hear others' messages. Listen to and acknowledge the entire message; then ask, "Is there anything else?" This will help you get to the real issue of concern and ensure you are addressing the true problem.

6. **A.** "If I understand you correctly, you are saying . . ." is a great way to validate another's story. Many times, misunderstandings or misinterpretations will be identified early on. Paraphrasing is an excellent communication tool to

improve understanding and reach mutually satisfactory solutions.

7. **B.** Beginning questions with *what, when, why, where,* or *how* encourages the other person to create an entire sentence and express a complete thought rather than providing you with only a yes, no, or grunt for an answer.

8. **C.** Air disagreements. Exhibit your commitment to finding a solution, and seek areas of agreement or missing information. Staying calm is an essential component to removing the stalemate.

9. **A, B, C.** All are reasons for and results of polished listening skills.

10. **B.** People who create positive connections are good questioners and listeners. Because of their developed communication skills, they can better handle the trials and tribulations they encounter. They have a real chance to maximize success through improved listening.

Quiz Scoring

Ten correct—Your listening skills are excellent, and you have become a good influencer.

Eight or nine correct—You know what you want, but can't always get a buy-in from others. Work on improving your own skills by practicing listening to someone speaking on television.

Six or seven correct—You need to focus on the other person and stop thinking about what you will say and how they will respond. You barely hear the theme of the conversation, so your responses are often not on target. Pay attention and listen up!

Five or fewer correct—Your listening skills need more work. Until you improve in this area by following the tips in this chapter, don't be surprised if you continue to have conflict and Toxic People in your life. Keep practicing; your skills will improve if you're persistent.

Three, Two, One . . . Blast Off

There are three levels of listening. The challenge is to create self-awareness so you know at any given point in time how you are listening. Knowing your own demonstrated level of listening will help prevent you from becoming a Toxic Person.

LEVEL III—LA-LA LAND LISTENING

Freda saw Marco walking toward her. Running the other way was an option, but she knew he would eventually find her. Sure enough, Marco approached and started talking. As he was speaking, Freda's mind was filled with anger left over from their last meeting. Marco was such a jerk! So uncaring! Didn't he realize how offensive he was? What a great time to confront him, she thought. No one was in the work area, and she could speak without worrying about observers.

Then Freda thought, "Why do I have to do this? Doesn't his manager see how he makes a fool of himself in front of clients and colleagues?" Marco finished his statement and asked Freda for her opinion. Instead of answering his question, she lit into him with venomous rage, only to be overheard by their manager, who was standing out of her line of sight. It was too bad Freda wasn't listening, because that was exactly what Marco was telling her!

> You cannot truly listen to anyone and do anything else at the same time.
>
> —M. Scott Peck, author of *The Road Less Traveled*

Listening at Level III means you just don't give a rip and have chosen la-la land listening. It is all about you. In your exasperated state, you wait for the noise to stop so you can tell your conversation partner what is wrong. Escalation of a problem or issue easily occurs. Decontaminating Toxic People is not even in the plan. Results? It makes matters worse and hurts the situation, often to the point of no return. Losing credibility, tearing down trust, and being seen as difficult to work with are often the outcomes of Level III listening.

In Level III listening:

∎ You pay attention only to yourself.
∎ You listen only to know when to talk.
∎ You listen passively without responding.
∎ You fake attention with occasional "uh-huh's" or nods.
∎ You make judgments and form rebuttals.

Judgment and spilling over with rebuttals is the focus of Level III listening. Ask someone—your friends and family—to give an honest evaluation. Are you ready to hear how bad you really are? I doubt it. Do you wait impatiently for the other person to finish so you can say what's on your mind? Many people listen for the noise to stop so they can begin their input, idea, or rant.

Expect to have misunderstandings and serious conflicts if you continue to listen at this level. Look in the mirror and you'll see the Toxic Person.

LEVEL II—SKIMMING

Monica was trapped in yet another customer meeting. She knew this would be a waste of time, because she had worked with the client before and felt she knew exactly what they needed. Her mind was racing with the prospect of calling a new client right after this meeting—one whose business could really put her in the spotlight. Her wandering thoughts made her miss a quick statement about the client's merger with another company; she also missed the directive about where to send reports and other information. Monica was thinking, "Same old same old. I'll just run the reports as I always do and that will give them what they want." Her failure to follow up as instructed led to a distraught call from the client asking, "Weren't you at the meeting? Didn't you know we wanted those reports send by courier, not regular mail? You have really messed us up, and we are not happy!" So Monica's time was spent resolving her mistake, costing her and the client additional time and energy.

Most people listen at Level II, hearing only bits and pieces of a given conversation. Level II listening means paying attention to what you want to hear rather than to what is actually said. Level II listening is pretending to listen with all the right cues to the talker: "Um-hm," head nodding, encouragement, and the like—but it's all fake. Your responses have little to do with what has actually been said. It is all about what you want to say and just a very small bit about what was actually said.

In Level II listening:

- You listen logically and to content only.
- You remain emotionally detached.
- You concentrate only slightly on what is said.
- You give others the false sense of being listened to.
- You hear the words but are not really listening.
- Your impatience becomes a barrier to good communications.

Level II is where most people listen the majority of the time. Because of their lack of attention to the message or the other party, conflict often ensues. Though better than Level III listening, Level II listening leads to problems, anger, and misunderstandings.

Franco had an employee, Jana, who wanted to speak with him. Franco always referred to her as "Jana the Star" because she was an excellent performer. As Jana entered his office, Franco motioned her to the guest chair. He hung up his phone and immediately turned to his computer, began typing, and then said, "So, what's up?" Jana explained that she was expecting a baby and was very excited. She relayed her plans for taking limited time off after the birth because her husband was choosing to be "Mr. Mom." She also outlined her plans to train her colleagues in keeping her files, to bring in temporary help, and to manage every detail. She insisted the group would not even know she was out for a couple weeks. All Franco heard was "expecting a baby" and his imagination ran wild. "Jana the Star" would be away and that meant his numbers would drop. He tuned back in when she mentioned her "colleagues keeping her files" and his thinking kicked into to the poor producers calling on her clients. His mind was screaming, "What a mess," and he did not hear the part about her real solutions.

Formula for handling people: (1) Listen to the other person's story. (2) Listen to the other person's full story. (3) Listen to the other person's full story first.

—General George C. Marshall, American
military leader during World War II

LEVEL I—TUNED IN

Joshua was always amazed at how Neil was on the leading edge of every conversation, especially if there was a problem or conflict. Neil quickly responded with thoughtful comments and turned even the most contentious situation into agreement.

Somehow Neil easily gained the buy-in of the group and even customers. Baffled, Joshua asked Neil how he managed to consistently get the results he wanted. Neil replied, "I learned early in my career that listening was an area of communication that I control directly. What amazes me is that more people don't get it!" Tough, though, he thought. I can only change me.

Neil was a Level I listener—he was purposely tuned in to the speaker. You can do this and effectively use your skills to decontaminate the toxicity of any situation. Paying attention emotionally and logically means listening between the lines. Use this stage of listening in every situation. Level I listening gives you the information you need to decide how much energy you want to put into the conversation.

In Level I listening:

∎ You refrain from judging the talker or the message.
∎ You keep an open mind so you can see the other's position.
∎ You stay in the moment so you can acknowledge and respond.
∎ You practice keeping body language open.
∎ You listen from the heart and are considerate.
∎ Your paying attention sends the right message.

When conflict is apparent, Level I listening is critical. Collaboration, understanding, and wisdom are enhanced. Problems are solved, creativity expands, and time is saved. After learning of all its benefits, the real question is, "Why don't people always listen at Level I?"

Be different—if you don't have the facts and knowledge required, simply listen. When word gets out that you can listen when others tend to talk, you will be treated as a sage.

—Edward Koch, U.S. politician

THREE LISTENERS

Amy sat in the front row of the lecture hall. She was interested in the topic, Gender Differences in the Workplace. Fred, the speaker, was given an introduction that was impressive. As he began, his initial example included the statement "Women take care and men take charge." After he used the term "he" in several sentences when Amy thought he should have said "he or she," Amy turned off and dismissed Fred and his remarks on the topic. She remained in her seat, mentally fuming and with a closed mind, not hearing anything else that was said.

Turning off your listening because of a few words that don't fit your likability index can create conflict and problems. Amy was tuned out and listened at Level III.

Sitting next to Amy was Gerry, who was told by his boss that attending this session on Gender Differences in the Workplace was mandatory. He was upset before he even sat down. Gerry knew he had to report back to his boss, so he took enough notes to get the salient points of the presentation. Fred, the speaker, was thrilled that someone was taking notes and misinterpreted what he saw as total acceptance of his ideas. Gerry did report back to his team and boss; however, he did not apply one idea and therefore continued having issues with his work team and other colleagues. Gerry was skimming and listening at Level II.

    Bill also was in attendance. As an employee of a very culturally diverse company, he decided to really listen and pay attention to Fred's delivery of Gender Differences in the Workplace. He was having difficulty relating to women, both at work and at home, because they sometimes seemed too emotional and took things way too personally. His focus on the message allowed him to hear the content and to choose the areas that could be best applied to his situations. Sure, Fred had some points that Bill thought were too "airy-fairy and fluffy," but he still listened. He walked away with new insights, validation of some of his own thinking, and a new perspective on creating better relationships with women. Bill was tuned in and listening at Level I.

Survival Tactics

You learn to listen by being quiet, both verbally and mentally. Stop trying to practice on living human beings. It doesn't work. What you do need to do to get started is choose a television program that features one person talking at length—a public affairs program, documentary, or lecture. I find C-SPAN to be especially useful for practicing Level I listening.

Here is the trick. Assume that everything you are hearing is true and don't judge the material. Every time your attention wanders, drag it back to the speaker. Do this for roughly half an hour every day. Initially you will have to pull yourself back into focus every one or two minutes. That's how bad most of us are at Level I listening. When you're feeling accomplished with this, begin practicing on human beings. And keep at it. Your tendency will be to drift off.

Want to have some fun? Pull some of your colleagues and work group members together and make a game out of it. I can tell you that some people won't want to play, and those poor sports are the ones who probably need it the most.

Result? Less conflict. Remember: Your right to respond comes only from your willingness to listen. If you don't listen, you're not ready to respond.

Listening skills are improved when you learn to be quiet. Yes, you have to listen to the tirades of Toxic People. Do not interrupt them. Do keep them on track. If they drag up old issues and examples that do not relate to their current theme, interrupt and say, "I want to know more about the issue you started with." Did you know that *silent* and *listen* are spelled with the same letters?

When people are having verbal temper tantrums, it is usually better to just let them exhaust themselves. They won't listen to you anyway, because their story hasn't been fully told. Be careful about using the suggestion of interrupting—use it only if they are way off track.

You have to listen. Usually you don't because you want to stay in your own little world and are too scared to step outside. Typically, you are not prepared to venture into other people's domain. Here's the rub. You could do a better job of seeing things from their point of view by simply listening. Open up and visit their world to see what it feels like.

Being responsive does not mean you have to *agree* with their situation or point of view. Understanding is not the same as agreement. People are entitled to their views and to have you listen to them without bias. Isn't that how you expect others to listen to you?

I was presenting my Toxic People keynote to a group of medical malpractice insurance professionals, and a woman approached me after I had finished. She brought up a problem she called Malpractice of the Mouth. (Perhaps we should call poor listening habits Malpractice of the Ears!)

Are some of your Toxic People just plain boring? Do you catch yourself daydreaming and your mind wandering every time they speak . . . and speak . . . and speak?

Help is near! Listening to people who are boring, speak in a monotone, or have nothing to say is frustrating. Use your skills to listen more effectively and keep them on track. Understand that it's the right half of the brain that tends to wander—the creative, non-linear side. The focused side of your brain is the left hemisphere, which contains the areas where words and language are processed.

Train yourself to say, "My mind will not wander, and I will give this person respect." Saying some kind of mantra forces you to the part of your brain where you hear words and solves the daydreaming dilemma. Using strategic self-talk moves your thinking from daydreaming to focused communication. Frustration is reduced, toxicity is held at bay, and you can move on.

Do you converse with people, especially the toxic ones, who go off track? Ramble forever? Make you crazy?

Try using one of these:

"Excuse me for interrupting. Is our focus right now _____?"

"I've lost focus on where we are. Do we need to talk about _____?"

Of course, these must be said with positive intent, a pleasant look, forward body language, and no sarcasm—all great survival skills if you choose to use them.

> Sainthood emerges when you can listen to someone's tale of woe and not respond with a description of your own.
> —Dr. Andrew V. Mason, author of *And or Love*

In conflict, speaking louder is often the approach used, whereas listening louder would solve so much more. So, stop being so self-absorbed. Stop using silence as the "when to talk" indicator. And stop blaming the other person for not listening to you, because you probably are not listening to them.

Did you know that listening is a real act of courage? You make yourself vulnerable when you listen, because you may actually find out you are incorrect. Someone else may have information that proves you wrong. This is a frightening prospect, and difficult to face. Your frames of reference may be torn down, and you may feel at risk when having to rebuild a new structure.

You are being very generous by being a good listener, because you are open to others' opinions and attitudes. Nothing can be more reassuring to another person than to be listened to in an attentive way, especially if you are entangled in a toxic situation. If you have someone in your life who nags, it may be that *initially* you did not listen to them. Nagging you became *their* survival tool. Stop the insanity and break the nagging cycle by spending time to find the underlying cause. Ask questions and dig deeper if you choose to give the relationship any focus or energy!

Huh? Your Challenge

Listen for a change. Amazingly, conflict is reduced, and many times Toxic People are even pleasant communicators.

Become a great listener. It will resolve toxic situations and separate you from the masses. Most people have no clue about the importance of this skill.

Here are six quick steps for great listening:

1. Have an open mind.
2. Stop talking.
3. Turn off your self-talk (see Chapter 14, "Mental Looting").
4. Start listening.
5. Ask questions to find out more.
6. Keep listening.

Sonia was tired of the skin rash on her arm, so she made an appointment with her doctor. He hardly took time to ask her what was wrong and gave little sign he was listening when she informed him she thought it might be something in the creams she was using. Sonia had changed brands several times but still had the terrible outbreaks. The doctor took less than a minute to look at her arm before pulling out his prescription pad. Sonia asked what the prescription was for, and he said, "It's for prickly heat." "Prickly heat?," she queried. "I thought that was from sweating. It's snowing, and I don't think I've been sweating since last summer." "Well, that's what it is," he said authoritatively. This was the first of five doctors she visited within a year to diagnose her problem.

Finally, Sonia found a doctor who listened to her situation and carefully examined her rash. Her problems were solved during that appointment, because he was able to hear her and then apply his knowledge and experience. "You are allergic to para-aminobenzoic acid (PABA), and many creams contain that ingredient. Just be careful when you choose body lotions and sunscreens."

Just think how good listening could improve your personal relationships. It's like the guy who complains that his wife always says he doesn't listen to her—at least that's what he thinks she said.

Start right now by paying attention to how you listen in every situation. Begin challenging yourself to go beyond hearing and really listen. Listen up!

CHAPTER 12

Control the
Uncontrollable

I I I

*The alarm sounded, the snooze button was slammed down, and Don-
ald turned over in disgust. He thought, "I hate my job. I hate my boss.
I hate my life!" This message played over and over in his head on the
trip to work. To validate his dismal message, the elevator's Muzak was
playing "Sad Boy" by Dorsey Burnette. "Ah, just the right music for
another day that will suck," Donald said aloud. Stressed before he even
started the workday, he felt totally out of control and had become a
Toxic Person.*

Donald was buried in a self-made hole. He was right about
the fact he didn't control his company, his boss, his job demands, working long hours, and the people he worked with. He
didn't even control the people in his personal life, including his
partner, kids, friends, and family. What he did control were his

choices in life. His mental terrorism was pushing him to be helpless.

Control Your Job

David Lewis, a workplace psychologist, found that working long hours in a result-driven workplace causes stress, anxiety, and depression in employees. The workers he interviewed agreed that the top three short-term effects of stress were increased irritability, undermining of work performance, and an increase in mistakes—otherwise known as toxic behavior.

So, who is in control? You are. The choice of accepting a position is yours (well, unless you are incarcerated, perhaps). No one is holding a gun to your head. The decision to work in a particular industry or study in a particular field is your choice.

Kay was a scientist for a major pharmaceutical company. Her job was interesting, and all of her university studies were being used. Challenging as her research was, though, she didn't feel a connection to her work. Guilt and stress were building as she thought about the possibility of changing industries and directions in her life. She did not sleep soundly, and dissatisfaction and unrest muddled her thoughts. This began to affect her work and relationships. She was becoming argumentative, withdrawn, and unfocused. She was becoming a Toxic Person.

After listening to many authorities about taking control of her life, Kay bravely decided to join an association that supported people aiming to do what she wanted to do. Having realized that being a professional speaker would certainly fulfill her dreams and help her live her mission in life, she faithfully attended meetings and participated heartily, but did not quit her day job.

The first step was finding a mentor who would guide her to what was real and true in the speaking industry. She questioned many people during the networking sessions and finally identified the perfect person. Kay referred to her mentor as a "gift from God." With help from her carefully selected mentor, a message was crafted and a strategy developed, and she was well on her way. Working on her self-confidence, focus, and next steps was often a struggle, but she pushed forward with the help of her mentor. She knew she was in control of her future and career and quit her day job!

Kay chose not to what-if her life away. Amazingly, many people remain in jobs they hate. Do you? I've heard every excuse, and one of my favorites is "I can't leave because of the pay." Most people think they are out of control when it comes to their remuneration. Wrong! You are in total control of how much you make.

Here are three reasons you use the "I can't change because of the money" excuse:

1. You *are* being paid too much for what you really do.
2. You have not taken inventory of your talents (or lack of talents).
3. You have no idea how to market yourself.

YOU *ARE* BEING PAID TOO MUCH FOR WHAT YOU REALLY DO

If you know you are being overpaid for your job because of company or industry wage standards, you know you will be out of that job soon. So start looking. In today's environment, every leader, manager, and supervisor is looking to cut costs, and the easiest way to do it is to dump the overpriced employees. Then the company can either hire less expensive labor or outsource the job. Fair? Maybe not, but it's business. Unless you own your own company, you are not in control of the bottom line.

Solution? Ask for more difficult assignments. Learn a high-level skill. Work harder and smarter. Keep a list of the all the skills you have. Without being a Steamroller or a Know-It-All, let it be known that you are capable of accomplishing more. Volunteer to cross-train others, lead an improvement team, or start a Learn and Burn lunch meeting.

The merger was complete, and Donna knew she was at the high end of the pay scale. Her job had been identified as redundant with another capable employee from the acquired company. Donna requested meetings with 10 of the leaders in the merged company's management team. Six of them set appointments with her.

Donna had just one question: What was the biggest issue they needed to address to quickly reach their united goals? The majority of the leaders told her that it was to address the clash of cultures in the merged company. On her way home from work, Donna stopped by the library and asked the head librarian for some resources to help her learn how other companies have addressed and solved this culture gap problem. Several books were recommended. She contacted the local junior college and developed a relationship with one of the business professors. After putting together a program in half-hour increments, she became a star with the leadership of the merged company. They knew she was worth every penny they were paying her.

Another idea is to take your skills outside the company. Teach literacy, make recordings for the sight challenged, or educate others less fortunate.

You do have some control over the perception others have of you. So if you think you're being paid too much, do something. If you don't, they will solve the problem for you.

YOU HAVE NOT TAKEN INVENTORY OF YOUR TALENTS (OR LACK OF TALENT)

Right now, without too much mental processing, write down the five reasons you are good at your job and why you should not be replaced. You should be able to spout these off as quickly as you say your own name. If you can't do it, I recommend keeping a talent journal for a few weeks or months. You are the one in charge here, so know what you do well!

> *Fritz had been wishing someone would notice his hard work. His last project not only was under budget, but the customers' expectations were exceeded. The president of his group, Jack, was coming to town, and Fritz thought to himself, "Maybe his visit is to recognize my efforts." The meeting began and everyone was filled with expectation. But what happened? The entire unit was recognized and Fritz was not singled out as being the real hero!*
>
> *After the meeting, Jack asked Fritz if he could see him in the conference room. Without advance notice, Fritz was asked, "So tell me: What makes you so good at your job?" Fritz was at a loss for words. He shrugged it off, saying, "Oh, nothing in particular," and lost the opportunity to reveal his talents. The next opening for a management lead was awarded to Fritz's cubical mate. Toxic behavior subliminally grew in Fritz's mind simply because he didn't speak up.*

If you inventory your talents and discover that you aren't as good as you thought you were, here are a few suggestions. You must continue to prove your worth. The level of employment or unemployment really doesn't matter; you are in control of continuing to prove the value you bring to the company. Toot your own horn, speak up, and do the best every day. If the company takes a new direction, implements new software, merges, or develops a new product, you are responsible for learning the nuances and mechanics of making it work. People who wait to be trained or communicated with will be on the chopping block.

So how do you keep updated? Do you Google your company to find out what is being said in the press? Do you pay for training yourself? Are you constantly looking at ways to improve your behavior and self-awareness? If you answered any of these with a no or not a definitive yes, you are in trouble. Sorry for the bad news, but this is the real world.

It may be that you are a pain in the rear. Do you bemoan policy changes? Are you part of the grapevine and catch yourself gossiping? Are you listening to others who are filled with negativity? Do you talk about anyone behind their back? If you said yes to any of these, you are on your way out the door. Companies will not embrace office politics that undermines their cause. They don't have to. What companies will do is promote people who produce, use fewer resources, manage conflict, work successfully with colleagues, find solutions, and move the company to success. This applies for all kinds of businesses; so don't argue that this is not your environment.

From government agencies to major corporations to entrepreneurs to service businesses, they are all in it for one reason: to make money. And do you think not-for-profit or educational organizations aren't part of this scenario? Think again. People vote on bonds to support your government and academic job. Folks donate to financially strong nonprofits, giving these entities the funds to support your salary.

YOU HAVE NO IDEA HOW TO MARKET YOURSELF

You are a commodity. Employers buy your talents because of how you have positioned or marketed yourself. What is your marketing plan? When was the last time you updated your resume? And if you did update your resume, do you understand the nuances of resumes in today's businesses?

In addition, you are in sales. Every time you open your mouth, you are attempting to sell an idea to another person or group. Challenge yourself to read or listen to a book on selling and marketing. You are constantly selling *you*. Update your references and your resume. You never know when you will need them.

Jan was very happy with her current position and was often told what an asset she was to the company. Her industry was on fire and there were so many opportunities, but she was satisfied to stay where she was.

One morning, her phone rang and she was greeted with an invitation from a well-known competitor to send in her resume that afternoon. The rival company had landed a very large client, and apparently they were desperate for her help and expertise. The caller said they would give her an extra two weeks of vacation annually, all the benefits they had to offer (which were better than what she was currently receiving), and a 40 percent pay increase. In addition, there would be a handsome bonus.

Jan really hadn't been looking, but couldn't resist the opportunity. There was one catch, though: the short deadline. Pulling her seven-year-old resume out of the archives, she quickly brought it up to date and e-mailed it over. The competitor company was disappointed to find it was obviously not what they wanted. Much of the terminology had changed in the industry, and the old worn-out terms stood out in Jan's resume. That was too bad. Jan lost out to another employee at her company who had chosen to take control of his future. He had trained himself to update his resume in all respects at least every six months.

Control Others

You can't change people, but what you can do is control the outcomes you have with them. Being the bearer of bad news is difficult, and probably you, like most of us, have been a wimp and an avoider who would rather do anything but get tangled in the confrontation.

I remember requesting to laterally transfer into an outside sales position from telephone sales. The manager who could make this happen said, "We don't have women in outside sales. We don't think the wives would like you traveling with the guys. In addition, you wouldn't always be home to cook dinner for your husband."

In the following days, I was seething but didn't confront the situation. Instead, I complained to anyone who would listen, creating a toxic environment. Every time I told the story, my rage would consume me. It never occurred to me to confront the manager who said I couldn't do the job. Shying away from confrontation meant I didn't have to face disagreement or difference of opinion, which I thought would lead to bad results—more misunderstandings, retribution, and humiliation.

What is the confrontation *you* could control but don't? Perhaps it concerns a colleague in the next cubicle who plays her music so you can hear it, someone who frequently tells offensive stories, or a coworker who constantly makes personal calls. You allow the behavior to continue even though it is driving you nuts. You feel totally out of control.

Here's how best to approach the confrontation. Ask for their permission before you get involved in telling them the problem.

One of the people you work closely with has toxic body odor. You are unsure of the possible reaction if you mention it. If you get permission to proceed to raise a difficult subject before you dive into the issue, odds are you will elicit a favorable response.

"There's something I've wanted to mention. I don't know if it's really my business to bring it up, but if it were me, I'd want someone to say something. Is it okay if I raise a sticky subject?"

You control *when* you will approach in most cases. Be sure to choose a calm moment for you and for the other person. If either of you is worked up over anything, postpone the conversation to another time.

Stay in control even if it seems a problem *must* be addressed right then. Simply say, "I need to think this through. Let's meet back in an hour to further discuss this." You are in control.

Control Yourself

The first order of business in managing Toxic People is taking personal responsibility for your own behavior. You *do* control the way you approach anything. The major culprit of a toxic office is you, and this is something you can control.

Remember, the only person you can change is yourself. Trying to change another person only makes for great first marriages. Don't get angry if you can't control other people, especially Toxic People, because most likely you don't even control your own behavior consistently.

You have the skills—you just don't use them. Much of what we've covered you already know. If you choose not to apply these skills, is it because you are lazy or because you just don't care? If either of these is true, don't complain, because you *could* change if you wanted to. It's something you do control. Interestingly, you find fault with other people because you won't look at yourself.

Control yourself and take personal responsibility for your skills. If you don't have them, do something—vow to become a lifelong learner.

Once, after completing a presentation, I was asked by the leader of the event if I could go home with him. Since that was not realistic, he encouraged me to write and record so people could extend the message. I still listen to my own downloads and CDs because even though I wrote the information, I sometimes forget to apply it. (Sign up for my free newsletter at www.MarshaPetrieSue.com.)

Then there is the flip side of this. An attendee at one of my presentations said, "I expected your information to help me in my work, not as a person." Huh? I had to write that one down. People continue to amaze me.

You do need to hear the message many times. When I find a book or CD that resonates with me, I will listen to it at least seven times. I've learned this is the only way to remember salient points and have them become habits.

FLUFFY SOFT SKILLS

Even though it is not easy to learn and use these interpersonal techniques, some people view this approach as fluff. Soft skills are hard! Interpersonal skill training is frequently deleted from organizations' budgets without even a second thought. If that happens to you, good. Spend money improving yourself and don't expect anyone else to do it for you. The only two helping hands you will ever have are attached at the end of your arms. My dad told me this when I was a teenager and I will never forget it. How about you?

Most people don't give a rip what skills they have, much less use—especially when it comes to soft skills. This is a painful reality for exceptional leaders and employees, because they know positive outcomes are derived from training in such topics as conflict resolution, communications, relationship management, listening, and more. You must take a new look at this training and dump the old moniker of "no value to investment" when it comes to training.

HERE IS THE PROBLEM

In many organizations, training employees to sharpen soft skills is analyzed as either an investment or a cost. How do you perceive interpersonal skill training? How does your company feel about this training?

Here is a new twist on why successful, profitable companies are training their people. Investment firms are looking at ongoing education as a reason to encourage investors to put their money in companies. How would your company do? Laurie Bassi, former professor of economics at Georgetown University and vice president of the American Society for Training & Development, found a simple solution. Companies should be required to report how much they invest in each employee.

Interestingly, when CDW Corporation's investment in employees was reviewed, the stock price was up by 50 percent whereas the stock market had gone down. The training investment is paying off because CDW recognizes that that training is an investment, not a cost.

Stock market pressure to reduce costs and increase profits isn't the only reason firms don't spend more on training, Bassi acknowledges. Many decision makers aren't convinced training is productive, or they worry workers will leave once they are trained.

These skeptics get two answers. Statistics-filled studies find that training does pay off. People like Laurie Bassi are putting their money where the facts are and investing in companies that spend heavily on employee training. When people are trained and know the company is working in their best interests, conflict and toxic situations are reduced.

This is laborious work, as most companies do not have this information readily available. The value of training is elusive. So here's what you can do. Bassi has found that the typical firm invests 2 percent of its payroll dollars in training. She looks for firms that double that investment in their people. The results for her Human Capital Portfolio are stunning: 24 percent annual return for the two years since she founded it.

Training is obviously something companies can control. If you are not the leader in your group, take this information to those in charge. I'll bet they don't even know about it. In my opinion, this approach will be effective only if you are investing in yourself. The concept is the same for individuals as for companies.

Control It All

There are six soft skills that reduce turnover, improve outcomes, and build profitability.

1. *Communication skills*—developing flexibility to others' styles. Provide training of leaders and employees to magnify the importance of personal responsibility by increasing self-awareness.

2. *Conflict management*—learning to use conflict as a brain-storming and creativity tool. Create mentoring and coaching opportunities for individuals struggling with interpersonal skills.

3. *Relationship building*—strengthening every person's diverse connections. Walk your talk, whether at work or at home, to become a better role model in relationship development.

4. *Team building*—building teams that function through chaos (too much to do and not enough time). You've got to decontaminate toxic teams, too! Provide team-building activities, whether through assessment tools, buying a cake for a celebration, or having a simple potluck.

5. *Empathetic listening*—hearing the message from every person and keeping an open mind. Learn to put your own thoughts aside, stop thinking about what you will say next, and really hear the concerns of the other person.

6. *Building self-awareness*—understanding individual prefer-
ences to heighten flexibility in all situations. Develop the attitude of a lifelong learner and read about human behavior.
This will help you both personally and professionally.

Having queried thousands of people in all types of organizations, I have found these six elements to be the resounding issues
that all employees want to improve. Many consider these to be soft
skills. As Daniel Goleman, author of *Primal Leadership* (Harvard
Business School Press, 2002), says, "If they do contribute to the financial strength of the organization, it becomes prudent to increase training budgets and engage every person in a 'winning
together' focus. The term of becoming a 'learning organization'
has never been more important."

MORE TRAINING = BETTER OUTCOMES

Training is no longer purely an operating expense. It is an investment to help leaders and employees hone soft skills. Daniel Goleman also says 10 percent of our success is because of cognitive,
learned skills, whereas 90 percent is because of emotional intelligence or our emotional quotient.

How do you rank in the training department? Do you invest in
your own learning? Do you uncover goals of others and help them
set a plan for their next educational opportunity? Does your company support a training perspective? Congratulations if the answers
are all yes. If not, what are you going to do? What suggestions will
you make? The excuse of "I have no control" no longer works. No
matter what your position, level, or experience, you are the one

who must take the first step. Soft skills are hard, and conflict resolution is at the top of the list.

If you say you don't have the time or the money, you are using excuses. You have the time and money to control more than you think! Copy what successful people do to take control of their situations. Only stupidity is original.

CHAPTER 13

Toxic Customer Service

■ ■ ■

Have you invested in your Toxic Check Meter? This is a noninvasive test providing immediate results to determine the intensity of your customers' anger. It lets you assess how ticked off they really are. It does not, however, determine the *cause* of a toxic customer's anger, as this varies by a subject's individual rage. Dream on—of course there is no such equipment. Wouldn't it be great if you could actually have tools that would determine exactly the kind of situation you faced? Actually, you do have equipment and it's built into your talents, skills, and behavior.

Government statistics tell us that one upset client can influence up to 67 others, whereas one great client will influence only three. Consumers relive and relay their experiences to others for

$22^1/_2$ years! If you are a business owner or have a job, this should be very scary to you.

Want to have some fun? Type "Customer service sucks" into your web browser search engine. At last count, there were 2,410,000 web sites, postings, and blogs outlining specific company names and problems. Is your company part of that list? Whether you are the leader of the company, on the maintenance team, or anything in between, you should be concerned. The minute a company heads downhill with poor customer service results, your job is in jeopardy.

Every employee, manager, and supervisor—everyone—has a responsibility to provide exceptional client care. The problem? You have to be "on" all the time for two reasons:

1. Everyone you touch every day is your customer, and I mean everyone. From the gardener to the grocery clerk, the doctor to the door attendant, your partner to your parents to your kids, they are all your clients. Now, quit laughing. You must hone your behavior and responses to be consistent 24/7. Taking personal responsibility for all your outcomes is the key.

2. It is the perception of the client that is important, and yes, the customer is always right. Of course, some people are not a good fit with your services and products, so you refer them to someone else who can build a better relationship. That means you may be giving your competitor business. You may lose great clients *and* employees to higher ground. If employees perceive that they are not being treated fairly, they will seek another position.

Toxic clients stem from toxic behavior, so always keep in mind how you would want to be treated if you were standing on the other side of the counter, or computer, or were at the other end of the telephone.

Winning Over a Toxic Client

Finding new customers takes capital resources and marketing; it costs approximately six times more to attract a new client than to keep one you have. When one of your well-earned clients is upset, a formal strategy must be in place. Employees must be trained, and toxic clients must be approached in a consistent manner. Here are the sacred six survival skills for handling toxic clients.

LET THEM VENT

You have to let them release the steam. Like a pressure cooker, if you take the top off without first letting the steam release, you will wind up with a mess! Don't try to resolve the issue without listening to the problem. (See Chapter 11, "Listen Up!," for listening skills.) If you do, it makes you and the company look bad, because the customer just gets angrier. Train yourself to really listen to their language. Keep them on track when their complaining starts to wander to information that will not help you determine what the issue is and resolve their problem. Try this language:

"I want to make sure we get this resolved quickly; so what we need to focus on here is _____."

"I want to make sure I understand exactly what I need to focus on here."

When they veer off track, wait until they take a breath and then come back with your input. Keep your tone low and steady.

Jasper opened his credit card statement and was furious. He grabbed the phone and dialed the customer service line. He screamed into the phone, "I didn't want this upgrade and am really upset it showed up on my credit card monthly statement. You people are idiots! I can't believe you cheaters would do this to me. This happened to me last year when I bought a gift for my wife. My son is an attorney, so you had better make this right. You have no idea how upset I am!" When he took a breath, C.J., the customer service rep, said politely, "I can hear how upset you are. May I have your account number and we will get this resolved right now?"

Toxic clients often have a difficult time getting their story and data neatly packaged. Your verification of what they tell you is critical.

Jasper continued to rant, "I needed this gift delivered before the holiday. We did change the size, but we didn't think this would affect the delivery time. You people promised me it would be here. I'm upset, my wife is upset, and my youngest child is very sad. This is my third time calling you! We want this resolved now!"

C.J. knew the best thing to do was to calmly paraphrase the issue and try to get the account number again. "I am so sorry your package was not delivered in a timely manner. Your account number should be on the right-hand corner of the statement, under the date. Can you give that to me, please, and we'll get this resolved."

YOU DO NOT HAVE THE RIGHT TO GET ANGRY BECAUSE THEY ARE ANGRY

When you get angry, they win. Period. You give your power away. Remember, the customers are the ones with the money, and they will choose to spend their cash elsewhere—so they win. Even if you are mentally upset but force yourself to be physically calm, the client will see or hear your anger immediately. People are smart and can see through the thin veneer of faking it.

Some customer service people—and perhaps that would include you—should be charged with arguing under the influence. There should be secret shoppers and customer service sneaks who call the poor behavior. When people do get caught supplying poor replies, the "consciousness of guilt" syndrome hits, and they become even more angry because they know they've been caught while arguing under the influence of not taking the proper approach. Here are some clues.

Don't say anything that resembles any of these statements:

"You have to . . ."

"You're wrong."

"It's against our policies."

"I can't help you."

"We never . . ."

"We can't . . ."

"You must be confused."

SEE THEIR ISSUE FROM THEIR VIEWPOINT

Convey to the toxic customer that you understand their situation. Remember you are not saying that you agree, just that you understand.

"I'm sorry about what happened."

"This must be very upsetting to you."

"I see what you mean."

"I can see why you feel this way."

"I can tell how frustrating this must be."

You need to convey that you are *genuinely* sorry. Mean what you say, because people can tell if you are faking. Check the tone of your voice if you are on the phone.

One of the ways to check yourself is to tape-record several conversations (just your side, because in most states it is illegal to tape both). Review this recording to identify any words, tone, or behavior that should be changed to wow every customer, whether angry or not, every time! It is your job to do this. I recommend taking this action for improvement every three months, if not more frequently.

Use this information in training others to help them learn *before* they have to encounter the same scenario. If you are doing this as an individual, get someone you trust to listen with you for another viewpoint. So many times you *think* you are saying the right words and in your head it *sounds* like your inflection is great, but others do not view it the same way. Their perception is different, so listen to what they have to offer.

In addition, when dealing with angry customers, beware of being trapped by their negative attack. The situation will escalate if you begin to mentally call them names such as jerk, stupid, creep, bozo, moron, pushy, turkey, rude, and liar.

Typically, if they are name calling, you will mirror what they are saying and react with the same. Don't fall into this trap. They want you to become angry, because then they have power over the situation. In addition, don't take what they say personally, because anger is a real in-your-face emotion. Screaming, rude comments about your mother, aggressive body language, and fist raising can make you either sink or attack.

PROBLEM SOLVE ACTIVELY

Immediately clarify the cause of the customer's problem. Ask yourself, "What does this customer need, and how can I provide it?" The quickest way to get here is to ask the toxic client directly, "What do you want me to do?" Whatever the client says is a starting point, especially if it is way off base as to what will really happen.

Don't jump to conclusions. Rather, ask questions that help clarify the cause of the customer's problem. Continue to dig by asking questions and paraphrasing the responses.

- Don't use their name too frequently. Think about how you feel when someone does this to you. Their toxic behavior will be amplified if you do!
- If their assertion is well stated and the conversation is flowing, let them finish two or three comments, *then* paraphrase. Their anger will heighten if you play their words back to them too frequently.
- Concentrate on listening. If you are taking notes, typing, or doing something that distracts you from the issue at hand, you are not providing the best in client care. I understand that in some circumstances you need to input the information on the computer, so just write down the key words and fill in the blanks later.
- Don't let your mind wander back to a similar scenario you had and how that was resolved. Stay in the moment. There

will be some part of their complaint that is unique and you will miss it if you are recalling the past.

When you have finished with the client, think about how you could resolve this situation so it will not be as daunting the next time it happens. Think about what you did well and what you should change next time to create a better outcome.

AGREE ON THE SOLUTION

Before diving into a solution, make sure you have all the facts. When you are comfortable, move on to the solution phase, and work with an *acceptable* solution to the problem. If you still do not know what will satisfy the toxic client and make them happy, simply ask. Don't second-guess what will resolve the issue, because every situation, and client, is unique.

If you cannot commit to their solution or wish, tell them that you find it necessary to verify the resolution and will be back with them and that this step will ultimately save them time. Here is the part that is very upsetting to me personally and I'm sure to many others: You are promised a call back, and never get one.

We needed a new wood-burning stove for our cabin. We went to Florence's retail outlet, selected a stove, and ordered it, paying half at the time of placing the order. Florence said she would call as soon as she received information from the factory about delivery time. Not hearing from her within a month, we called her back. "Well, I still haven't heard. I think they must be really busy."

Were we concerned? No. However, another 10 days went by without a call from Florence. We phoned her again and she said, "They start production in another month for the stove you ordered." We didn't believe her, so we called the factory ourselves. What a surprise when we found out the stove was in stock and were able to arrange to have it shipped to Florence's retail location. Even though her company eventually properly installed the unit in the cabin, neither my husband nor I will recommend her. Ever!

Always follow up with the answers and solutions when you say you will, even if it's a call to tell them you know nothing. Do you want to create toxic clients? Leave them hanging with no solution or information.

FOLLOW UP

What impresses me is when a company actually follows up after I've had to contact its customer service. Interestingly, some companies even provide this service after you order from them. One vendor, PrintingForLess.com, not only gives me excellent pricing and products, but the follow-up is amazing. I receive a phone call verifying that I am satisfied *and* an e-mail. When its competitors call me and say they can beat its prices, I really don't care because I am so impressed with its customer care.

Reverse the Scenario

The decision to adopt a cat was a big one for Janita because she owned her own business and did a bit of traveling. After carefully determining that she could give a cat a nice home, the attractive, blond kitty lover decided to visit the Pet Shop because it was "Adopt a Pet Day."

Barry introduced Janita to Joan, the person in charge of adoptions. Janita explained excitedly, "I want to adopt a kitten or a cat today." With one look at Janita, Joan announced, "Well, I'm not going to let you adopt one. We do not want flight attendants adopting one of our precious animals." Startled, Janita protested, "I am not a flight attendant. I'm a business owner and—" Joan cut her off. "I'm not going to argue with you. You aren't getting a cat today." Again, Janita started to speak. "I really—" Joan cut her off again. "Well, I'm not letting you have a cat. We do not let your kind adopt our animals." Shocked and disappointed, Janita left the pet store.

In reviewing the situation with a friend, Janita realized she had an idea from the moment she saw Joan that the experience was going to have a bad outcome. She later recalled hearing Joan's loud voice berate another Pet Shop associate as she entered the store. Joan's demeanor was aggressive, her voice was laced with anger, and her approach was antagonistic. Janita's internal Breathalyzer was working, and perhaps she should have just left before the entire scene played out.

If you apply the skills and ideas covered in this book, you will be able to activate your internal Breathalyzer without even thinking. Evaluating people and situations before you are intertwined in anger, conflict, and discord could prevent stress for you and your work group.

External and Internal Testing

Every office should have toxic police who have the right to accuse people of being TUI—talking under the influence. Leaders and managers need to give Toxic People a Breathalyzer test and challenge the behavior of those creating havoc. But who creates the toxic behavior?

Have you given yourself a Breathalyzer test lately? Do you really know how you react or respond to Toxic People? You have absolute control over one thing, and that is your thoughts. This is extremely significant as well as inspiring and terrifying to most people.

All a Toxic Client Wants Is . . .

- Timely service.
- Fast response.
- Knowledgeable customer service reps.
- Advice and counsel when appropriate.
- Accuracy.
- Consistent service.
- Fair pricing.
- Courtesy.
- Promises kept.

CHAPTER 14

Mental Looting

I I I

Mental looting can provide initial paralysis during the decontamination process. The input from others becomes disturb-
ing and creates a thought process that ignores reality and generates
mental terrorism. This human mayhem can be overcome by finding the true underlying cause of your thinking.

The internal hurricane of self-doubt mentally loots you of
your confidence, willingness to accept change, and ability to deal
with Toxic People. Your frames of reference create unconscious
patterns from very small bits of experience. These translate into
the memories of negativity, can make you a victim, and create internal misery.

Look to Ben

When you are having trouble moving forward, stop and create a so-called Ben Franklin list comprised of the pros and cons of the situation. This neglected tool helps you survive the floodwaters from others or even from yourself. When making this list, brainstorm with yourself and include everything. Nothing is sacred!

Problem: I need to approach my boss and explain that I am stressed and have too much to do.

PROS (REASONS FOR TAKING ACTION)	CONS (WHY I THINK I SHOULDN'T)
My work will be better prioritized.	The boss will get angry.
I'll have less stress.	The approach will create more stress.
I'll be more productive.	Because I brought it up, my boss will give me more work.
I'll determine a better use of my skills.	My boss or team doesn't care about my being overwhelmed.
I will have better focus.	They won't see how my focus will be improved.
I'll take on projects that are more relevant.	They may think I am currently assigned the right projects.
My leadership will be noticed.	They will blacklist me.
I'll go to lunch with friends.	I have no friends. It doesn't matter.
I'll leave work at a reasonable hour.	They won't think I'm doing my fair share.

You now have a list that will help you *realistically* evaluate what you are facing. When you are feeling mentally drained, try this and you will find that it works very well, especially if you are stuck and can't find the momentum to move. If you don't take action, *you* will become toxic because you feel trapped. Always ask yourself, "What is the worst thing that can happen?" This question can put an overwhelming task or issue into perspective.

Stephen was upset with his peer, Norm, once again. They shared the same office space, so it was hard for Norm not to overhear conversations. Stephen had worked to improve his relationship with Laura, the office manager, but had again argued over how the supplies should be ordered. Once Stephen hung up the phone, Norm turned around and started gossiping about Laura and giving Stephen advice, emphasizing how poorly he had handled the call. Flipping his chair around, Stephen worked for the rest of the day in total silence, not saying a word to anyone. Fuming for hours didn't resolve anything, though, so the next day Stephen had a plan. If Norm thought he had all the answers, Stephen would approach him over a cup of coffee, and they would put together a pros and cons list. At least now he had a plan.

This process will accomplish two things: make Norm part of the solution, and take a fresh approach to managing the Laura situation.

Toxic Soup

Rescue yourself! Run away from being ill-prepared, because you do have untold resources at your disposal. You can quietly supersede the lethal toxic soup fed to you.

Here's something you can do, as you are personally account-able for taking the heat out of the toxic soup. Use the freeze-frame technique to reframe negative thoughts into positive ones. Catch yourself midsentence and midthought, and take a positive spin ver-sus a negative twist. Freeze the toxic frame of reference. This can be done no matter how daunting and toxic the situation.

Learn to quietly supersede the negatives in life. Get out of be-ing trapped into calamity thinking. It vandalizes mental capabil-ity. Survive the floodwaters from others by choosing not to be a victim. Your suffering from the initial paralysis caused by others and your own thinking can be changed. And don't ignore reality. You have untold resources at your fingertips. Use them and stop making excuses.

Where is your focus in difficult times? Beware! Sometimes the focus is on the storm rather than the gorgeous rainbow after the weather passes. Are you thinking about how catastrophic the out-come will be, or do you give yourself a clear view of how you want it to be?

Peggy was late for the meeting. Screeching into the parking lot, she saw one space left. "I'll just pop around to the other side and get that space," she thought to herself. Out of the corner of her eye, she noticed a massive SUV speeding into the same lot. Just as she was aiming her car toward the space, the SUV slammed in front of her and took the space. "You idiot! You jerk!" she said out loud.

At this point, she knew she could either throw the toxic soup into her thoughts and feed on it or choose to find a parking place on the street. Her friend called it "parking karma," and she turned her thoughts to how the exercise of walking from the street would be good for her because she would be sitting for the rest of the day. "It's the

*world's way of making sure I burn a few calories," she thought to her-
self. Freeze-framing her negativity and focusing on the meeting gave
her a new objective.*

Only you can take personal responsibility for learning how to
decontaminate toxic people by becoming a great internal communicator. Hang around positive, supportive people, and dump those
who mentally loot you. You do not deserve their toxic waste. Some
people use their verbal weapons to loot your self-esteem and self-
confidence.

If you catch yourself focusing on the incoming storm and the
what-ifs, ask yourself, "What can I change and learn?" Arm yourself with 24-hour awareness of your self-talk, because you do become what you think about. Whether at work or at home, your
behavior will change only if you constantly work on it. So, don't
just try something once or twice! Practice and upgrade your internal and external communications. Record your external communications and review them.

Yes-o-Meter

We earlier identified "yes" behavior to be found mainly in the
Needy Weenie in Chapter 7. Have you bought into having a yes-o-
meter? Society today has a plague of yes people, and this creates
toxic situations and people. Saying yes is not exclusive to these people, however.

Most people hate confrontation and conflict as being related to
rudeness and discomfort. I'll bet you have a real fear of that short-term

unpleasantness of telling someone "No," and to avoid it you are willing to subject yourself to the ultimate unhappiness.

Have you ever said yes to:

- A volunteer job you knew you didn't have time for?
- Helping with the blood drive at work?
- Attending a meeting that you knew would be a waste of your time?
- Going somewhere you really didn't want to go?
- Buying clothes you really didn't like?
- Participating in an activity that you hated?
- Buying equipment because you didn't want to hurt someone's feelings?
- Having a drink when you really didn't feel like it?
- Eating something that you knew you didn't care for?
- Going for coffee with someone you really didn't like?

This is the ultimate in mental looting! For example, if you have too much on your plate because of constantly saying yes when you should be saying no, this will push you into becoming a Whine and Cheeser (Chapter 8).

How about getting run over by a Steamroller (Chapter 3)? They constantly throw too much at everyone—except for that one person who has learned to say no.

Perhaps we should consider the behavior of the Zipper Lips in Chapter 4. They mentally loot you because you've stopped even asking them to do anything. Their endless pauses and lack of input are making you crazy. In frustration, you wind up doing it all yourself.

You are in the habit of saying yes to just about everything because this response is easier than coming up with a reason for refusing. Think about a difficult project that you know is underfunded and not well thought out. You will say yes to being on the team instead of asking questions and finding out more. As you get busier, the problem intensifies because it's easier to slide along with the status quo. The result is you question your own thought process and mentally loot yourself!

How to Say No without Feeling Guilty (or Getting Fired)

Learn to have a better score on the yes-o-meter by using the following three-step model:

1. Acknowledge the request or action you are being asked to do, and paraphrase what they want delivered back to them. This clarifies expectations, because people don't always communicate well.
2. Use "I" language and take personal responsibility for what you need. (I think, I need, I want, I feel, etc.)
3. Give the person requesting you to do something two choices (when possible) and let them choose.

Manny had told his boss, Robin, that he had to leave at 5:00 P.M., his normal departure time. The day progressed and at 4:45 Robin walked in with a pile of work. Pushing the pile closer to Manny, Robin said, "I need you to finish this work before you leave today."

Manny said pleasantly, "This project must be important to you. As I mentioned this morning, I need to leave at five o'clock today. I am not able to stay. I can check on whether someone else is able to stay and help, or I will rearrange my schedule for tomorrow morning and help you then. Which one of those two is going to work better for you?"

Did you just faint? Are you saying to yourself, "No way! I'd be fired!" Pay attention to why some people don't stay late. Listen to their language, and you will find that they use this kind of approach. Understanding, practicing, and using similar language will help you teach other people how to treat you. And you do teach people how to treat you.

I would recommend writing out exactly what you want to say using the model. Practice it many times and get to know the structure, flow, and words as well as you know your own name. Keep practicing the words, because in your first few tries using this method the outcome will not be exact. If you don't take this advice, you will continue to fade and say "Yes" when you know you should be saying "No!"

Defensive People Are Looters

People who always jump back and say "I knew that!" exhibit defensiveness. Dealing with defensive people is not easy and is truly a learned skill. If you don't learn it, they will mentally loot you. Face it. People will get angry, whether your partner retreats to silence or a work peer starts yelling. These behaviors may seem to be different, but they are not. They are both defensive. Someone who chronically makes fun of others also shows defensiveness.

The first key is not to protect yourself. They don't care about you, and your behavior can push them even further away. If you start to retreat into your own kind of inappropriate behavior, you are allowing them to mug you and steal your self-worth. Remind yourself that this is their way of defending themselves *and* it has worked so well they continue to use it. You reward them when you allow them to pilfer your confidence.

To prevent this theft, work on always being a good listener. Listen intently and hear their words in spite of their emotions. Summarize what you are hearing to stay on base. If they drift to another topic, draw them back to the key point that initiated the defensiveness. If you don't know what is going on, listen more intently and ask "tell me more" kinds of questions.

Arguing

Take a hard look at how you argue. Everyone has had an argument that they were sorry for and walked away from feeling awful. Your first strategy should be to make sure you are arguing about the same issue. It is your job to confirm this.

"Don't argue with an idiot. People watching may not be able to tell the difference!"

When you argue, you give reasons or cite evidence in support of an idea, action, or theory, typically with the aim of persuading others to share your view. Some people argue just to cause havoc and to make others feel bad. Mental looting is often the result of arguing because you are not confident enough to stand up for yourself.

The budget had not been approved, and Tim needed to move forward with his project. When he approached Mona, his superior, to determine budget approval timing, she slammed down her notebook and said, "Look, Tim, I'm not going to argue with you about the budget. I'll get back to you when I have more information! Now go be productive and stop your whining."

Tim was devastated. His hands were tied and he was unable to move forward with this critical project. How would he tell the team that they were at a stalemate? His confidence was at an all-time low. That evening, he surfed the Internet for ideas on problem solving, negotiating, and debating. After reading a few articles, he had new assurance on how to proceed.

He went back to the team, and they revisited their strategy for completing the project. They established a new methodology and a new budget. Presented with the refreshed direction, Mona had new energy in understanding their monetary needs and promised to revisit his revised scenario. Tim's passion to move forward was reignited, and that was obvious to the rest of the group.

Generally, to get what you want, you need to negotiate with other people. Improving your communication skills (i.e., improving your arguing skills) will help. To get what you want is one reason for arguing. Other reasons to argue are to find out what you believe and what other people believe and why.

Keep an open mind to differing opinions because it:

- Shows what position a person holds.
- Allows others to present their points or perspectives.
- Helps arguers reach and understand new views and reasons for those views.
- Does not mentally loot people.

Set your ego aside and look for truth or at least discover different ways of researching issues and situations. Listen carefully to arguments presented and formulate your own response. Too many people just knee-jerk and don't *think* about their response and the impact it can have on the other person.

People also need to know that you understand their frustration and their reason for being pushed over the edge. That means you do not raise your voice, use intimidating language, or display other hostile characteristics; you merely agree on the issue. And never call anyone names. This is a real sign of immaturity when people resort to name-calling.

Remember that this is understanding, not agreeing. There's a big difference!

Counseling and Coaching

One way to mentally loot other people is to keep them in the dark. The lack of information, especially when it concerns the quality of their work, borders on inhumane. If you wonder why morale is in the pits, this can be the reason.

Whether you are a worker bee or the leader, it is your obligation to review job responsibilities. I learned early in my career to make sure each person understands their job responsibilities by reviewing everyone's job description at least every six months. This recap includes the rewards of doing the job well. I then ask *them* for the consequences if they do not meet those job definitions and expected outcomes. Have your pen and paper ready. People are often much harder on themselves than you would be. Listen carefully and note down what they say.

I call this "Rewards and Consequences." Down the road, if you then have job performance issues, you have a list of exactly what should transpire. Their defensiveness is better managed because there are no surprises. What could they say? They set up the consequences! Of course, this approach is used within the parameters of your human resources policy.

> When Barbara was hired, her boss, Tom, reviewed all the assigned job responsibilities. He then told her all the payoffs for Barbara if she did her job and even if she exceeded the required outcomes. She was thrilled knowing that she could get a raise and be up for the prime assignments, time off, and even a promotion!
>
> Then Tom got out a pad and pencil and said, "So tell me, Barbara, what should the consequences be if you do not achieve these targets?" Without even taking a breath, Barbara said, "I should be fired." Tom reared back and said, "Whoa—I was thinking that before that happened perhaps there could be some cross-training, outside coaching, or attending a workshop. Let's design this together." And they did. In his leadership role, Tom had learned that people were much harder on themselves than he was. Also, there was no question as to what could happen if the outcomes were not met. Reviewing the job responsibilities, rewards, and consequences with all

of his employees every six months was at the top of his leadership list.

If you are the employee, it is your responsibility to check the expected outcomes of your job with your boss. In today's crazy work environment, many managers and supervisors do not take the time to tell you what *they* want you to do as well as their perception of expected outcomes. If they don't have time to meet with you, write out what you think your job responsibilities are and give them the list for their verification. This way you have documented what the parameters of the job entail. This is your personal responsibility to understand, so stop saying, "Well, they didn't tell me." In addition, if you are surprised by negative comments in your annual appraisal, you need to validate what your leader expects of you. Schedule this in your calendar for a quarterly review and remember you are the one who takes the lead by requesting the meeting. Of all the research I do as a professional speaker, the number one concern with both leaders and employees is the lack of communication. If you are not in the loop, take action to find out what you need to do in your job. If you choose not to, don't be surprised if you become the Toxic Person and feel mentally looted.

Asserting Yourself

Learning to assert yourself in a positive way, without hostility, is the approach to take to ensure a better result. Controlling your anger does not mean ignoring the situation. If you choose to retreat, you give the other person control over you and the outcome.

> Jeb was reporting to the group on the project Marina and he had completed. This was a critical turning point for the success of Marina's largest client. But what was happening? Jeb was presenting the findings without acknowledging her contribution. Jeb had done this before, and Marina had approached him with her concerns. She thought this had been resolved, but obviously it had not. The client was pleased and thanked Jeb for the outstanding contribution made to the very sensitive project.
>
> When Jeb's presentation was finished, Marina stood up and firmly stated, "I want to thank Jeb for delivering our results. Spending equal time in developing this plan was a real pleasure, and I'm pleased with our solutions. Please let Jeb or me know what questions you might have," and she calmly sat down.

Marina stated her thoughts without being hostile. What would you do in this situation? Feel mentally looted, sulk, or seethe at the next meeting? If you choose to become defensive and hostile, you look like a poor sport. To stand up for your rights takes confidence on your part and the knowledge that you do have the capabilities to drive the outcomes you want.

Some situations *do not* deserve your energy and concern. When you determine the best solution is to walk away, do it, and feel good about your decision.

Don't let anyone break into your mental state and loot the richness of your productivity and power. Some people who do this have been mentally looted themselves and therefore view the looting behavior as acceptable.

Don't let them come back to you and say, "Oh, I was only kidding. Don't take it so seriously." Reviewing Chapters 3 to 8 and the possible responses will serve you well. Mental looting is serious, and you have to prevent these felonious attacks on your thinking.

CHAPTER 15

Toxic Infections

■ ■ ■

You are contaminated every day with toxic infections derived from people, jobs, or your environment. This realization occurred early in my work life.

Upon graduating from college, I took a job as a kindergarten teacher. This was before kids had the opportunity to go to preschool, which meant that most of the kindergartners had not developed social skills or become used to sharing. The noise level every day was earsplitting and my time in the classroom became a challenge, but the worst part for me was the parents.

Seven-year-old Joe was selfish and rude. In approaching his parents to see how we could work together to help the child, I was shocked when they went on counterattack and screamed, "You're ruining our child!" I wanted to reply, "Well, you've done a pretty good job yourself!," but didn't say so. They spewed their toxic venom and infected me with total distaste for my chosen profession. That was just the first incident of many.

I hated every day, crying on the drive to the school and on the way home. Some evenings, I would sit in my car and sob because I didn't want to go back the next day. For those of you who are teachers, God bless you. It just wasn't my forte, desire, or passion. I had a terrible toxic infection, and it had happened because of my choices.

After six months, I decided to start looking for something else. Scanning the want ads, I saw an ad for a "candy girl" who would provide free samples of goodies at retail locations. I was a girl and I liked candy, so the interview was a no-brainer. I got the job and loved it. I was healed! We allow ourselves to become sick, and it is our job to change the environment.

Awareness is key. I began to notice that my original profession had not been the only toxic infection I was experiencing. A symptom I should have noticed was the toxic soup being dished up by one of my acquaintances. For example, this was the comment I had received after explaining my job predicament: "You want sympathy for your choice to be a teacher? Look up *sympathy* in the dictionary, and you'll find it right along with *shit* and *suicide*." I've never forgotten that conversation, as it left a real scar in my mind; but it was the bad-tasting medicine I needed to move me forward.

Taking a cut in pay was worth it to free myself from the emotional angst of teaching, not to mention eliminating the excruciating migraine headaches. Little did I know that this choice to change was the beginning of a successful career in sales and marketing, so I am grateful for all the cuts and bruises I've endured. I was *healed* from the toxic infections.

Moral of the story: If you are in a job you don't like or if it isn't what you want to be when you grow up, change it. However, here is the rub: You *must* do the best job you can in the moment, right now and today. Don't become a slacker, because then you will be spewing the toxic soup on your work group and on your employer. They may call 911 (human resources) and give you DNR (Do Not Resuscitate accompanied with a termination notice), and you will be out the door! You are the doctor who will take charge of your career and professional success.

Triage: Are You Infected?

The constant flood of stress chemicals and associated metabolic changes that accompany unmanaged anger and toxicity can eventually cause harm to many different systems in your body. Some of the short-term and long-term health problems that have been linked to unmanaged anger and the absorption of Toxic People's venom include:

- Headaches and migraines.
- Digestion problems.
- Abdominal pain.
- Insomnia.
- Increased anxiety.
- Depression.
- High blood pressure.
- Skin problems, such as eczema.
- Heart attack.
- Stroke.

"We've known for at least 20 years that people who have chronic anger are more likely to have severe blockages in their heart arteries, to develop heart disease over time, to have increased risk of cancer death, and to have more rapid progression of arterial sclerosis, even increased risk of workplace injuries," says Redford Williams, MD, director of the Behavioral Medicine Research Center at Duke University Medical Center and a leading expert on anger management.

Norma is living proof of what toxic infections can do to you. In 1990, she was hired by a company that was willing to pay her big bucks to re-organize a poorly producing segment of the organization. She did not know that the situation was about as toxic as they come. After a few short months, her health was a mess and she had developed open sores in her mouth. Her physician thought it was thrush. "What? Isn't that what babies get?" she exclaimed. The doctor wrote her a prescription for a miracle drug, which gave her no relief.

Doctor number two, an eye, ear, nose, and throat specialist, diag-nosed acid reflux and assured her that was causing the sores in her mouth. Norma had waited two hours in his office, and the stress of waiting worsened her toxic infection. This physician prescribed a differ-ent miracle drug, which provided no relief. The open lesions were be-coming more painful.

Doctor number three (now six months into this), another eye, ear, nose, and throat guru, said a blood test was in order. The expert told Norma, "It looks like an immune deficiency—something like AIDS." In her mind, she had herself eulogized and buried.

Doctor number four, a dermatologist who came highly recom-mended, looked in her mouth and said, "It's easy to see that you have Hashimoto's thyroiditis. This malady is the most common type of au-toimmune thyroid disease. It is found mainly in women, although I have seen several men with the same condition. It occurs when the body's immune system becomes misdirected and attacks the organs, cells, or tissues that it was designed to protect. It is caused by not managing your stress."

Toxic behavior, both yours and others', creates stress and consequently ill health by spewing the hormone cortisol into your system. Norma's doctor went on to explain that if she didn't take charge of her stress, her condition would get worse. Lowering the cortisol level is accomplished by adding balance to your life, eating properly, and exercising regularly. It's just that simple.

Healing Toxic Infections

Times are tough. Trusting others is down, while blaming is up. Optimistic outlooks are down, and fear is up. Managing stress and healing toxic infections requires a blend of energy, humor, spirit, and self-confidence. Where will you focus? What can you do to move to a less toxic environment? Like Norma, you are the one who must take care of your health. Stress and unmanaged toxic infections will kill you.

ENERGY: A CURE FOR TOXIC INFECTIONS

How do you create energy? When you feel especially alive, what has occurred? When you feel stressed, what has occurred? My energy comes from feeling that I can handle any situation or person and that I am in control. Some parts of life you control: food, lifestyle, knowledge, time, relationships, appearance, thoughts—just to name a few.

Typically, you do not control others' perceptions, the weather, other people's problems, travel delays, poor service, or traffic. When you spend precious energy trying to control elements that are beyond your control, you feel down, out of control, and toxic.

> *The new team Francis was assigned to never seemed to do anything right. His attitude was in the pits, and he was procrastinating about setting a meeting with this dysfunctional group because he was convinced it would be another waste of his time. His energy to move forward was totally gone.*
>
> *He caught himself in this negative spiral. Keeping a journal and tracking what was making him nuts and what gave him energy helped him analyze the situation facing him. Francis learned that he must take the time to evaluate each of his teammates and understand what behavioral types they were, the payoffs for them, and the approaches he could use. (Refer to Chapters 3 to 8 for the types of Toxic People.) This gave him the stamina to schedule the meeting. In reviewing his notes before the meeting, he was confident that his relationship management skills were well developed, and he was ready to proceed and bring the much-needed energy and focus to the team's success.*

Here's the lesson. Francis could have become the victim of circumstance in this new assignment. As he did, *you* need to evaluate *your* situation by keeping a journal of what you learned and what you could change for next time. Check out your energy gains and drains, and control what you can.

Fact: People have been put on this earth to push your buttons and burst your bubble. Have you developed interpersonal skills to deal with these turkeys? Have you trained yourself to set up a reflector panel so your energy is not totally zapped? If they turn up the heat in the oven, your goose will be cooked if you don't take control.

Cure: Listen to people who motivate you. Yes, I know you've heard it all before, but do you really apply this technique with toxic infections? You are the only one who understands when you are sick of your environment and of the people who transmit the bug. Constantly listen and watch messages from different resources. Life is hard, and going it alone is difficult and can make you feel abandoned. Visit www.MarshaPetrieSue.com for suggestions.

SPIRIT: VIVACITY, VERVE, AND ENTHUSIASM

Spirit drives toxic infections away. Do you have real enthusiasm in your interactions with others? Spirit is built by caring and learning from your environment and not being engrossed only with you and your surroundings. This latter behavior is just selfish, because it's all about you. Surround yourself with positive quotes, goals written as affirmations, doable action plans, and positive people, and your spirit will soar. Enthusiasm for life is the key. Spirit is something you control.

Tips for building your spirit:

- Stay hopeful.
- Take risks.
- Volunteer for two hours a week.
- Celebrate with your family.
- Enjoy the outdoors.
- Share a positive thought.
- List reasons for gratitude.

Develop something you can say to yourself that is inspiring—perhaps something you write yourself, a poem that is important to you, or a list of quotes that move you forward. I believe it is a good idea to change yearly to give a fresh view to your spirit. I had originally read the thoughts in my daily affirmation in Larry Winget's *Shut Up, Stop Whining, and Get a Life.*

Here is my daily affirmation:

This day I give back more than I've received. I connect my head and my heart with my mouth. I surround myself with people I respect and who respect me and live by the law of attraction. My calendar is full of events that bring me joy and happiness to others. I have an abundance of money, and before spending I ask myself, "How much is enough?" I am thankful for my life and appreciate all that I have.

What do you do to strengthen your spirit? Did you know that online there are more than 1,970,000 blogs on enthusiasm? I believe it is because people know they need enthusiasm to manage all the negatives that come their way!

SELF-CONFIDENCE: HOW YOU VIEW YOUR ABILITIES

Popeye is right: "I yam what I yam." How you think about yourself either builds you up or tears you down. Your self-confidence is a result of your thinking; in banking terms, it is the emotional depository. If you view your abilities favorably, you've made a deposit into your account. If you berate yourself with self-deprecating self-talk and external comments, you are subtracting positive perspective from your emotional depository. Toxic infections make huge withdrawals from your self-confidence account.

This ultimately is how people view you. Feel good about yourself? The turkeys will have a difficult time getting under your skin. Emotional depository low? Those birds will have you on the platter and will be carving you up into little pieces.

Here are five ways to build self-confidence awareness:

1. When you lay your head down on the pillow at night, think of five great events from the day. You will wake up refreshed and rested.
2. Remember that you become what you think about. Dump the negative mind-set.
3. Get proper rest and exercise and start eating more healthily. And start today.
4. Do not let pettiness at work, at school, or in your personal life maintain power over your success. It will suck the life out of you.
5. Create confidence in your talents, and you will manage change as a fact of life.

Self-confidence is the cornerstone; if it's low, you feel vulnerable, your immune system is weak, and you will have toxic infections. You cannot decontaminate Toxic People if you feel the least bit toxic yourself. When you are vulnerable, you can count on several responses: Your thinking becomes clouded, you lose perspective, your self-confidence dwindles, and it is difficult to be objective about yourself and the situation.

Here are five tips for building self-confidence:

1. Maintain a strong belief in your own competencies to stop the thoughts of weakness, defenselessness, and helplessness.

2. Review your talents and build from your strengths. Check your weaknesses, and if they are the problem, learn to change them.

3. Keep your focus on being solution oriented rather than danger oriented. Understand that there is a problem to be solved, not a threat to your life or well-being.

4. Rise above it. Pretend you are in a hot air balloon, and lift your thoughts over the issue to get a new view.

5. Picture what you want versus what you don't want. Beware of becoming a self-fulfilling prophecy and falling victim to people and situations.

HUMOR: THE BEST MEDICINE

> "Laughing stock: cattle with a sense of humor."

Cure your toxic infections with laughter. We take ourselves way too seriously. The challenge is to put the humor back into your personal and professional life. Rent a fun movie like *The Jerk* with Steve Martin or find an old rerun with Bill Cosby. Take it to your next meeting and play a part that you find fun and humorous.

> "Energizer Bunny arrested; charged with battery."

Toxic Infections

Life is serious business, but don't take *yourself* too seriously. No one else does. Laughter creates endorphins and defies the stress hormone, cortisol, in your system. Stress hormones make you sick and give you serious toxic infections. When you laugh, you release the stress-buster endorphin hormone. This natural pain reliever is like a magic potion concocted in your body, and the dosage can be purposely prescribed by you. You may have heard of "runner's high," euphoria that develops in long distance runners as endorphins release and block out any feeling of pain.

Learning how to manage the level of endorphins in your system can cure toxic infections. According to the online resource WebMD, the release of endorphins can be attributed to exercising regularly, eating small amounts of chocolate, sunbathing (without getting burned), laughing, being massaged, meditating, singing, and listening to your favorite music.

When the turkeys have you in a neck hold, the stress hormones are taking over. Jesse Pittsley, PhD, president of the American Society for Exercise Physiologists, states, "For people who are physically active on a regular basis, they have active relaxation—by focusing on the sensation of moving your body and getting into the rhythmic activity and motion, it produces this relaxation response, and that I think contributes significantly to the feelings of psychological well-being."

The substances that your brain produces depend in part on your thoughts, feelings, and expectations. If your attitude about an illness or about life in general is negative and you don't have expectations that your situation will get better, your brain may not produce enough of the substances your mind needs to create a more positive results. If your attitude and expectations are more positive, your brain is likely to produce sufficient amounts of the substances that will boost your body's healing power.

Depression Infection

Feeling depressed lately? Job got you down? You're not alone. According to a recent International Labor Organization report, "depression, anxiety, stress, or burnout" is increasing, affecting (or maybe infecting) 1 in 10 workers in Finland, Germany, Poland, the United Kingdom, and the United States.

The study also found that in the United States, the treatment of depression costs between $30 billion and $44 billion annually and results in the loss of approximately 200 million working days each year. This is very sad, not to mention very expensive.

The main toxin, besides cultural and economic issues, is the development and rapid growth of information technology. With accelerated competition and the need to constantly keep up, the ability to break away and relax has almost evaporated. Personally, I love technology—*when it works*. When it doesn't, I start singing "If I Had a Hammer," the song by Pete Seeger and Lee Hays.

So, what's the solution? Get a new hammer? "Bring a dog to work" week? Office massages? Casual attire? But wait, there's more. How about a Jacuzzi in the break room, a chef to cook meals, and an in-house gym? Actually, these ideas are exactly what companies are considering and implementing for their employees to heal the toxic infections that contaminate offices (well, maybe all except the hammer).

The reason people bring dogs to offices is that they're working 75 hours a week and have no time to raise a pet. You've probably also heard that pets have been found to be natural stress relievers. Personally, I was raised without the dog gene and with the baby boomer work ethic of all work and no play gets you promoted, so I have an aversion to pets running around the office.

However, as most industries start looking for ways to trim budgets, it is a good idea for leaders to think twice before abruptly doing away with weekly massages and gym passes. These extras might actually be saving the company quite a bit of money.

Healing your toxic infections is your choice. Every situation — even a negative or poor outcome — can have a silver lining. Learn to blend energy, humor, spirit, and self-confidence, and practice keeping yourself out of depression. This combination is the prescription to make those turkeys more palatable and for a happier you.

CHAPTER 16

Ruffled Feathers

▮ ▮ ▮

Ruffle

1. To bother or fluster somebody.
2. To act as a source of irritation or annoyance.

Most of us can recall times when people ruffled our feathers, upset us, or ticked us off. But why do some people never get bothered, upset, or bent out of shape? They have learned to apply conflict management skills when events could otherwise make them distressed.

If a veterinarian sees a bird with ruffled feathers, the vet knows something is wrong and the bird needs care. As human beings, studies now reveal that anger and conflict release a toxic hormone, cortisol, into our systems (see Chapter 15). If this is not managed, you can become seriously ill; you can even die. Read on to learn specific ways to use Toxic People survival skills when conflict is in the roost. There is no reason to feel caged!

Caged?

Hello Marsha,

I met you at a conference and I thoroughly enjoyed your presentation. I am in a predicament of sorts. My office leader is a woman who is in her 60s and is a fast-paced worker. She is not business savvy yet she is good at her job. However, she mumbles and isn't clear with her instructions.

When I make a mistake, or am one in the chain of people who have made a mistake, she constantly reminds me of that, even in front of my boss. Having human relations training, I know this practice only serves to cause divisions in the workplace.

I also need to approach my boss about making necessary changes. Under this woman's leadership, or lack thereof, everything is very disorganized and messy. No records of phone calls are kept. Files are scattered. And not everyone in the team knows the status of a project or is aware of issues.

Communication sucks. I'm working in an office where I need to walk on eggshells. This woman is resistant to change. The lead person is 75 and ready to walk out if things get worse. And we have a new girl who is very smart and savvy, and I fear if we treat her poorly or do not back her up and put her intelligence to use, we will lose her. And I'm afraid that if I push for change I'll be viewed as a complainer, get set up to fail, be forced into a confrontation, and be fired. It has happened to me before. I can't keep losing jobs, but I'm sick and tired of working for bosses who don't care or are incompetent managers.

I/we need the boss's support and leadership. Yet, he knows squat about our business and is admittedly hands-off. How should I approach him? How should I ask him to stop this woman's finger-pointing and negativity? I'm in a position that if she quits then I would have the freedom to organize the office and make everything work like a well-oiled machine. Until that day, though, I feel powerless and frustrated, fearing that a goof-up due to poor training by this woman and a hands-off boss will cost me another job, and possibly a good marriage.

Another thing is that my wife and I own a little web site design business and we work from home. Our kids will be in school next year, and we'll have an opportunity to grow our business and go full-time. However, we need to triple our workload. And until then, I need this job. The pay is good, and it keeps a roof over our heads. What tools do I need to practice patience and achieve excellence at this position until I can get out of there and apply my energies to my own business? Part of the reason I want to work for my wife and myself is that I'm tired of dealing with Toxic People in the workplace. They have repeatedly ruined a good thing. And yes, I've been toxic, too, I admit.

Thank you for your help!

Matt

Here is the response from me, the Decontaminator of Toxic People:

> *Thanks for using "Ask Marsha" from the web site. Here are six suggestions concerning your question. I'll be interested to hear your input on them.*
>
> 1. *Approach your leader and tell her that you need her help so you can be more productive and make more money for the company. Take the pressure off of her and put it on yourself.*
> 2. *Ask her how she wants to be communicated to and when. If she wants to know why, say that you understand how precious her*

time is and you want to be efficient on the initial request/ process/project.

3. *Tell her you would like her to set some informal ground rules with you to make sure you are doing your best. If she doesn't, here are some suggestions: First, paraphrase and make sure you understand what she needs; her confirmation of the information will allow you to expedite the needs of the company and the client. Second, set a time, either daily or weekly, that is your time to clarify any questions about what is on your plate. This will help you stay clear and focused to make the best use of your time.*

4. *After you meet with her, take time the following day to thank her. This will verify that you mean to keep to the rules of engagement.*

5. *In every approach you make to her (or anyone else), engage with positive intent. Don't dwell on the past and what has not worked! Move forward in a positive, disciplined fashion.*

6. *Become a role model and never speak poorly about her to anyone (except your wife, and then give yourself only 10 minutes to vent— and move on!).*

I hope this helps. Let me know if you have additional questions! Cheers and good luck.

Marsha

If you are an executive, manager, or supervisor, your goal should be to continually learn and polish the skills necessary to work with people more effectively. In the example, Matt's office manager is toxic in his perception. Your challenge is to determine how people perceive you. You must learn to smooth ruffled feathers because of industries' ongoing issues with dynamic growth, unannounced change, reduction in workforce, and needed productivity. These factors and more continue to exert pressure on your capabilities as a leader. In addition, reducing turnover and attracting the best employees in your industry are enhanced by the reputation you create as a boss.

I recommend using the Skills Scorecard to determine blind spots that you may have.

Skills Scorecard

	GOOD WORK			NEED WORK	
	1	2	3	4	5
1. Have an optimistic outlook.					
2. Be a good communicator.					
3. Build relationships.					
4. Utilize delegation.					
5. Provide feedback.					
6. Allow mistakes.					
7. Be a role model.					
8. Respect everyone.					
9. Have realistic expectations.					
10. Set goals.					
11. Share information.					
12. Celebrate attempts.					
13. Manage conflict.					
14. Be open to learning.					
15. Be innovative.					
16. Celebrate wins.					
17. Say "Thanks."					
18. Show appropriate emotions.					
19. Choose issues carefully.					
20. Be a team player.					

For a copy of this scorecard, e-mail me at Information@Marsha PetrieSue.com.

Make several copies of the scorecard. The first copy should be scored by you about you—and be honest. What is the perception you have of how you work with people, lead, manage, and supervise? When scoring is complete, determine what three areas you do best in, and continue to focus on these as the good skills you have developed. Also determine the three areas you would most like to improve and circle them. Put this copy of the scorecard in a safe place.

Take 10 or so copies of the blank scorecard and distribute them to people with whom you work. Ask each person to complete the scorecard honestly and anonymously (one of the group can gather the completed scorecards and return them all to you). Look at the scoring others have done and see if there are any gaps between your perception and theirs.

Those blind spots are areas for you to work on, if you so choose. One thing is guaranteed: If you choose not to address the differences in perception, you will continue to ruffle feathers. Most people never want to "scorecard" themselves because they are afraid of what they will find out. How about you?

The retreat for a prominent law firm in the Northwest had begun without the attendance of one of the lead attorneys, Hampton. The retreat needs analysis completed by the employees of the firm revealed that there was unmitigated tension caused by the missing attorney. Hampton was arrogant and rude, and really didn't care what others thought of him.

The entire firm was still reeling from his most recent attack on one of the paralegals, Anne, whom he fired for no apparent reason. Two of the secretaries walked out that same afternoon because they couldn't take the ongoing tension caused by Hampton's upsetting behavior. Due to its high turnover, the firm was having a difficult time recruiting new employees and attorneys. Plus, its terrible reputation of having a toxic environment was jeopardizing client relations.

The managing partner was determined to solve this problem, so Hampton's behavior led the agenda items. However, after much discussion and review of the high-level clients Hampton had, the group decided not to broach the topic with him. Because of his enormous number of hours booked, the value of his clients, and the profits he brought in, they decided to maintain the status quo.

Feathers continued to be ruffled in the law office. Clients started to leave as the customer service rapidly deteriorated because there were not enough employees to cover the work that needed to be done. Within a year, profits were off and the leaders knew they were in trouble. A multinational organization purchased the firm, Hampton was fired, and the remaining employees were thrilled with the merger.

Moral of the story: Never allow anyone's inappropriate behavior to go unchecked. Whether you are the leader or an ordinary employee, you have a choice on what you can do! Use a scorecard or other assessment tool (DiSC, Myers-Briggs Type Indicator, Tracom Group's Social Style Model, etc.). These tools help you understand your personality and what is behind what you do, and give you a clue to your habitual patterns of behavior. Assessments help you find different ways to adapt and to solve problems. In addition, they provide a road map to help you (and others) with personal development. This is one of the reasons I became qualified to administer the Myers-Briggs Type Indicator. When a client has ruffled feathers, or if the client just wants better performance, we review each individual, then look at the team as a whole. It is good to know that 80 percent of the Fortune 100 companies use these tools to keep their groups on the cutting edge.

Don't whine or complain about another person—do something to manage the situation. If you are a leader, train yourself and your people in conflict resolution and anger management. It is disgusting to speak to a group whose leader claims to be too busy to attend. What kind of sign does that send? What it does is ruffle the feathers of those attending. Managers often consider themselves to be part of an elite group and think they are beyond learning because, obviously, someone noticed their talents and they were promoted. The outcome they receive is often a surprise to them and quite disconcerting.

Some leaders' efficiency in ruffling employees' feathers creates wrongful termination lawsuits, sexual harassment complaints, and other legal issues. The following four suggestions comprise a very short list of options for leaders:

1. Be an excellent listener. Listen between the lines. Practice in your professional and personal life. Be a great role model, constantly teaching others to listen more effectively.
2. Pay attention to the words you choose, and be flexible to the other person's style. It isn't all about you; it is all about them.
3. Take time for everyone. It is your job to pay attention to their concerns. The struggle you have is to be an excellent time manager. Learn to set ground rules that include particular times of day that work for your open-door policy.
4. Help people focus on the problem *and* the solution. Make it easy for them to complain and to bring you solutions. *Never* shoot down their ideas, no matter how bizarre. They usually see more than you do.

Conflicts, when effectively dealt with, are great opportunities for growth—both yours and theirs. You may know the skills for doing so, but can you apply them consistently?

Take the emotion out of whatever the situation is. The worst thing you can do when dealing with a conflict is become defensive or angry. If you start feeling upset, excuse yourself for a moment, count to 10, and return when you're feeling objective again. Or reset the meeting by saying, "I need to give this some thought. Can we resume our discussion tomorrow morning?"

Find the common ground. We have a tendency to focus on things we disagree on, which is counterproductive. If you think about it, there's always a lot more we agree on than we disagree about. When you acknowledge commonality, you instantly defuse the situation. Here's the rub: Some people are so used to getting poor results that the model in their head pushes their behavior to negativity and being ruffled.

Give objective criticism. People will be more inclined to come to you with problems if they feel that they are appreciated and taken seriously. That said, praise them when they come and talk to you about hard issues. Appreciate the person, challenge the issues, and bring about change.

Are you still dreading conflict? Like most people, you find it easier and more comfortable to stay upset than to resolve the situation. The reason is that it takes hard work to resolve difficult situations. If you have the internal resolve to make your life better, go for it and unruffle those feathers.

You either love people or try to control them. There is little room for anything else, and it is easier for you to control them than to love them!

Women Take Care; Men Take Charge

Traditionally, men were socialized to be independent. Playing competitive sports, learning to be in control was the message they heard in their formative years. Women were raised to build relationships and develop connections. You know the hunter-gatherer theories: men hunt, seeking out something specific, and women gather, bringing people or things together.

As a man or a woman, there are approaches you should use that work and skills that make for better rapport. Learning the gender differences helps you unravel one more piece of the Toxic Person puzzle. Men and women in today's business environment do not like to admit that there are approaches that work better with one gender than the other. Whether you're working from the glass ceiling or the cement floor, here are some considerations.

What women need to do in the business world when working with men:

- Do not minimize your accomplishments at work.
- Keep discussions focused on job-related issues or news events.
- Lower the pitch of your voice.
- Get to the point and include who, what, when, where, and how.
- Do not use tag endings, such as "isn't it?" or "right?"
- Drop your tone down to make a declarative statement.
- Monitor your head-nodding and smiles.
- Do not apologize unless you are wrong.

Melissa was an up-and-comer. She had been hired because of her excellent people skills and education. Though she was young, she had already developed a real command with managing teams. Her vice president, Laurie, wanting her to succeed, suggested they mentor together. Melissa was thrilled.

Laurie had already had feedback concerning Melissa's high-pitched voice, which made her sound like a little girl. The other team members were challenging her credibility, and her valuable input was not being taken seriously. Bob, the team lead, avoided interactions with Melissa altogether. He wore hearing aids and it was impossible for him to hear her because her high-pitched voice was out of his range.

In approaching her, Laurie suggested working with a voice coach. In just three sessions, there was a noticeable difference in Melissa's voice. Their next challenge was to help her stop ending sentences as though they were questions when they should be spoken as statements. Her coach told her, "Many women fall into the imposter syndrome. You look in the mirror and say to yourself, 'Someday they will figure out that I'm not a good as they think I am.' This is a result of low self-confidence, and it displays itself in your speech pattern."

Melissa had had no idea of this and was eager to continue her voice improvement work. During her lessons, she was also told that women use approximately five times more words than men. She worked in a male-dominated environment and knew she needed to be more concise and use less verbiage. It was hard to constantly focus on both her delivery and number of words. However, her peers soon began to accept her for the contributor that she was hired to be!

Moral: Record your voice. Listen to the inflection, authenticity, excitement, and commitment you have to the topic while checking the impact of your message. Whether you are male or female, if you don't like your voice and tone, change them. Focus and discipline are all it takes.

What men need to do in the business world when working with women:

- Use more terms of politeness like "Please" and "Thank you."
- Do not be afraid to ask for help—forget about your ego.
- Provide more facial and verbal feedback.
- Make more polite requests instead of barking out commands.
- Control your temper and handle yourself in a professional manner.
- Do not address women with condescending terms like honey, sweetheart, babe, or dear.
- Do not interrupt or monopolize conversations.

No one wanted to work with Eric. He was loud and rude and seemed to live on the edge of being toxic. He liked working with Joanie because she was smart and quick. In approaching her about the new project to which they had been assigned, he bellowed, "Hey, sweetie, do you have time for a quick drink after work? I know your partner won't care. He must realize what a package you are! That will give us some downtime to really get to know one another so we can speed up this project." He gave her a wink and a hug, barely waited for a response, and said in parting, "Great—see ya in the lobby at 5:15."

Joanie's friend overheard Eric and bounded over to her desk. "How rude was that? You're not going to meet that dork, are you? What a loudmouth! If I were you, I would prance right into our manager's office and scream sexual harassment. Don't let him get away with that kind of behavior!" Uncertain, Joanie just shook her head and went back to answering her e-mail.

Moral: The perception of a situation lies in the hands of the person being approached, not you. Ruffling feathers can happen without you even knowing!

Toxic E-Mail

Has anyone ever sent you an e-mail that upset you? It happens every day in the workplace. The sheer volume of e-mail is staggering: Every day 8 billion e-mails are exchanged on the Internet, and it is estimated that by 2010 this figure will have increased to over 42 billion. Consumers are expected to receive an average of 1,400 pieces of junk e-mail every day!

In your haste to read through and answer many of the received e-mails, scrutiny must be taken to ensure your reply is without words that the recipient will perceive as "flaming." Perceptions differ, and your meaning may lose its true intent as a person with a potentially different frame of mind reads it.

Qualcomm, Inc. released a version of its popular Eudora e-mail program that introduced an optional feature called MoodWatch, which scans both incoming and outgoing e-mail for "potentially offensive language" and rates it:

One chili pepper: "Better hope you know the person."

Two chili peppers: "Watch out, you're playin' with fire chilies here."

Three chili peppers: "Whoa, this is the kind of thing that might get your keyboard washed out with soap."

MoodWatch is based on theories developed by David Kaufer, head of the English department at Carnegie Mellon University. Kaufer conducted a study of flaming, which he defines as "computer-mediated communication designed to intimidate the interlocutor by withholding the expected courtesies of polite communication." Flaming is aggressive, angry, or rude language shot across cyberspace at the recipient. This has "toxic" written all over it! And you don't even have to see the whites of their eyes. You are out of range, so they can't strangle you. (Google MoodWatch for more information.)

You may think of flaming as just using all capital letters. Not anymore! You create toxic situations by the words you choose and use.

It is interesting that Kaufer's study is based on an analysis of over one thousand e-mails, producing dictionaries of flaming words and phrases that MoodWatch uses in rating individual messages. Of course, the usual profanity and offensive language will be left out for the faint of heart. Some other phrases, however, trigger a "chili alert" simply by their intimidating tone (examples include "I am not about to . . ." and "I'm sick and tired of your . . ."). I'll bet you rarely use those under-the-breath statements in person, but have put them in an e-mail! Cyberspace makes your unsuspecting recipient an easy target. The dialogue can go back and forth, raising the conflict, reducing trust, and throwing toxins on the situation.

Ruffling people's feathers through offensive e-mails is not necessarily done consciously. Even the language that you consider benign can come across as flaming. The styles of communication can be different, the perception of context misinterpreted, or the individual temperaments worlds apart. Layer on gender differences, generational divides, and cultural diversities, and you can have toxic interpretations. Get out your Hazmat suit to manage the toxic e-mail!

> *Walter was responsible for getting a project completed that was behind in delivery. He knew it was late and felt awful about the missed deadline, especially because he was the contact with the client. In a fit of haste, he sent out the following e-mail: "Albert, when is the project going to be done?" Albert became extremely angry as he read the message. "Who does Walter think he is? Who does he think I am, Superman?" To Walter the language seemed innocent enough. The sender knew the context in which the message was sent. So, the flamer successfully ignited the flamee, and all because of the stress and tension being felt by both Walter and Albert.*

Problem: Even the MoodWatch resource would have a hard time identifying Walter's e-mail as a "three chili peppers" alert.

Why do you need this kind of software, anyway? Because hiding behind the security of the keyboard has become an everyday event. The challenge is to send no more than three e-mails to manage an issue. Beyond three, you need to pick up the phone.

The responsibility should not be put on software, but rather on your shoulders. In this fast-paced, multitasking world, sometimes the obvious is not done. If you do not have software available to catch your misspeaking, then think before you hit that "can't turn back now" button known as "send."

Your personal responsibility extends to and through the send button. If your messages elicit negative reactions and responses, don't point fingers elsewhere. Check your wording carefully for those toxic words. Is there even a slim chance any word can be perceived differently than your intent? Create a keen awareness to this.

Whether you focus on gender differences, your leadership, the e-mails you send, or any other means of communication, put yourself in control. And you must make an effort to understand how others perceive you. Neither you nor anyone around you needs to have ruffled feathers! It's for the birds.

CHAPTER 17

On a
Personal Note

▮▮▮

Deanna lived with the threat of weekly migraine headaches. She had married her college sweetheart, Terry, immediately after gradua-tion. However, this union did not provide the kind of life she had dreamed of. His excessive drinking and job-hopping created turmoil in their relationship. Terry's Jekyll and Hyde personality had him jumping from being a Steamroller to being a Know-It-All. His belit-tling pushed Deanna's confidence to a low ebb. After considerable therapy with Dr. Bob, Deanna learned that indeed she had some choices. She decided to leave Terry, ending the toxic infection she had lived with for 11 years. Miraculously, her migraine headaches disappeared for many years—until she infected herself with another toxic situation.

One Day at a Time!

I, Marsha Petrie Sue, am a recovering Toxic Person and am challenged with managing my own poor behavior and making good choices about those with whom I interact. My mother was very sarcastic and could shift from being a Steamroller to being a Backstabber. Dad was a Know-It-All and a Zipper Lip, depending on the situation. It is our job to identify the Toxic People and take action, both professionally and personally. Don't blame anyone else—just take control and change it.

Who raised you, and how would you characterize them? *You* developed *their* behavior whether you wanted to or not and are challenged with their impact on a regular basis. Think about how you react or respond.

Toxic situations and people don't happen just at work and on the job. They can permeate every moment of your day.

Early one morning I was driving from Tucson to our cabin in the Arizona White Mountains. The long drive ahead reminded me that I really needed a cup of coffee, and there in front of me was a McDonald's. The street construction made it difficult to find the entrance, and then I was greeted with about a dozen cars in line at the take-out window.

Somehow I missed the little box you talk into to place my coffee order. When I arrived at the pay window, greeting me was a young girl who looked like she had just gotten out of bed and showed up, bad attitude and all. She said, "You didn't place your order at the box, so you have to get out of line and go the end of the line and talk to the box."

I asked, "Do you answer the box calls?" "Yes," she snapped sarcas-

tically, "but you *are not on the screen, so you have to get out of line and go the end of the line and talk to the box."*

"No, I will pay you and pull forward," I said. *As though she was preprogrammed, she said, "You have to get out of line, go the end of the line, and talk to the box." I could feel myself going to that ugly place in my brain, the Toxic Person box. Calmly, I said, "Now, we don't have to get your manager, do we?" With a deep, deep sigh she replied, "Just give me your money and pull forward." So I did.*

Arriving at the next window, I was greeted by a friendly, happy young man. I apologized for "being off the screen," and he said that it happened all the time because of the construction. I suggested to him that he go train the pay window girl because she was nasty, unfriendly, and an overall pain in the rear. His reply? "Oh, she always has a hair in her biscuit."

The moral of the story? Don't put up with other people's bad behavior. When you do, you give them the message that it is okay to act awful. It is not okay! It should be your quest to have good behavior yourself 24/7 and to expect it of others. Perhaps this is unrealistic, but we need to work on this as a team. Learn the skills to combat Toxic People, and don't allow them to hook you into their ugliness.

Toxic Kids Learned from Toxic Adults

How about toxic kids? My view is that parents today need and want their children to be their friends. The whole parent-child relationship is gone. Teaching kids behavioral parameters seems to have disappeared from the Mommy and Daddy files. I'm not suggesting that you revert to the June and Ward Cleaver days of *Leave It to Beaver.*

The techniques used so far in this book should be Parenting 101 training. Yes, I know what you are saying to yourself: "You never had kids! Who are you to tell other people how to raise children?" I'll tell you what I do know. Studying behavioral perspectives has been a passion of mine for over 30 years. When I see these preteen and early teen girls dressing like hookers I am appalled. I asked one mother if she shopped with her daughter when she bought clothes, and she assured me, "Of course. Doesn't she look cute?" I did say that I thought her clothing was a bit old for her age. I choose to not even try to change anybody and to leave them alone, but sometimes my curiosity just gets the better of me.

Parents today, I believe, are living vicariously through their children. It's a shame, because I think the lack of behavioral parameters jeopardizes the development of a healthy human being.

Al, my husband, lost his wife to cancer when she was 34 and he 35. Their children, Karen and Al III, were 13 and 14, respectively. With this terrible tragedy facing the family, he sat down with the teens and explained the new rules. "As you know, I travel just about weekly. Here are the rules: no booze or drugs. If you are arrested, don't use your last dime on calling me, because I'm not coming. You know better and your mother deserves better than to have you misbehave and screw up."

Al had new rules, too. He had to learn to cook, clean, be both parents, and more. This was the perfect opportunity for any bereaved family to become toxic, but they chose not to.

Now in their 40s, Karen and Al III are successful adults. It was not an easy road for either of them, but the rules were the rules.

They *knew* when they messed up and what the consequences were. No surprises.

I'll say it again: Life is hard. Life is not fair. Get over it!

Staying upbeat in challenging times requires a blend of energy, spirit, self-confidence, and humor. Perceptions must change, including acquiring a broader knowledge and a more comprehensive view. What is your perspective on life and the world? Do your lenses and filters of life include a wide-angle lens, or do you use a microscope with a narrowed view? Do certain situations and events create hostility in you and you drag it around like a sad sack?

Penny was a real dynamo. She woke up smiling and filled with life. Her family often questioned her to determine what she took during the night and she would answer, "I have a zest for life. Why not? The alternative is boring. I don't want to be on my deathbed saying, 'I could have, I should have, I might have.'"

Her spirit helped her live the life of her dreams. Many years before, a very negative aunt had influenced her. Nothing was ever right, and people were always wrong. Penny decided never to allow her life to fall into that kind of rut.

She knew life was not perfect, and when faced with difficult times, she dug for the lesson to be learned. Penny had to dig when her father passed away. He died unexpectedly in his sleep. After much thought she came to see the suddenness of his death as a true blessing, because he had never had to endure a sick day in his life. Even though her grief was deep, she moved on.

Her mother's fate was much different. Her mom had heart problems and was trapped for years in a wheelchair in a nursing home. The lingering illness took a toll on Penny, though she was always positive when she spoke with her mom. She would muster up a sunny outlook from the very bottom of her soul, knowing it would help them both.

Like Penny's aunt, there are some people who walk into a room (the Whine and Cheeser or the Needy Weenie) and drain the spirit right out of everyone. They are not fun to be around.

Patricia was down and out again. Her car had broken down, the cat was sick, and she had bought the wrong kind of coffee at the market. Plus her neighbor always parked too close to her car, the gardeners didn't cut the grass right, and the garbage pickup was a day late. The traffic seemed to be increasing in her neighborhood, there were lousy vegetables at the market, and her cleaning wasn't ready. To make matters even worse, it seemed that her friends were avoiding her, her boyfriend hadn't called, and her mother was always complaining. What was she to do? Life just wasn't fair, and she knew it would get worse before it got better.

It's Okay to Laugh at Yourself

Gerta was a crazy kid. She always was showing off, especially when she had an audience of her friends. Jimmy had built a makeshift go-kart with a motor. Taking the neighborhood kids for rides was his real pleasure. It was Gerta's turn to ride, so she hung onto the roll bar while the go-kart sped around the block with Jimmy driving. As they whipped by the spectators, Gerta decided to jump off right in front of the group to show how cool she was.

She didn't understand the physics of throwing herself off the moving go-kart, and actually thought she was going to land on her feet. But she skidded along the pavement, leaving much of the flesh from her arm and leg on the street. Her friends ran to her aid, screaming at her to determine if she was okay. Gerta looked up casually and asked, "Well, did I look good jumping from Jimmy's go-kart?" They all

laughed. That was her nature, and even as an adult she held onto find-
ing humor in just about every situation.

Don't Become Toxic When a Loved One Dies

The only part about getting older that I hate is that you start losing people who are important in your life. Here are my rules:

- Before they die, tell them you love them.
- It's not about you. It's about them.
- If you have fired family or friends from your life, it's okay. You should have had a very good reason at the time. Just be gracious.
- Be sad and know in your heart you will miss them, but don't mourn too long. They wouldn't want you to.
- Don't expect anything to be given to you. Stuff and money are not important. Just be glad you were part of their lives.
- Know that everyone grieves at different rates, so don't be upset if someone is sad for a shorter or longer period than you.
- Always do the right thing. Visit people before they die.

Karen Young is my stepdaughter and a real jewel in our family crown. When her grandmother, Lola, was ill, Karen spent endless hours car- ing for her with the rest of the family. Losing Lola, the matriarch of the family, was difficult for everyone, especially Karen because her mom had died when she was 13. Some relatives became toxic, while others, like Karen, decided to take a different path. Karen went to Lola's to help with cleaning out the home. That is never a fun task. Here are Karen's rules for cleaning out the attic:

■ *Don't have an attic.*
■ *If you do have an attic, don't store anything there except your Christmas tree.*
■ *If your clothes won't all fit in your closet, you don't need all those clothes!*
■ *If you store things in your attic because you don't use them but they have sentimental value, please realize they are one relative away from being at the dump.*
■ *If you think you're having a bad hair day, go clean out the attic. You'll realize your hair didn't look so bad when you started.*

Take Personal Responsibility for Kids

If you are a parent, take responsibility for your kids. It's not the school, the computer, the neighborhood, their friends; it's your responsibility to build their character, ethics, and manners. Teach good integrity and model it. Take total responsibility for the kind of human being your child has become. If you are a grandparent or have never had children, know that you are a role model with *everything* you do.

■ You are the parent and they are the children until they are 18.
■ You are in control and it is your money funding their existence.
■ Don't overload their schedules.
■ Teach them how to have quiet time and why being bored is good.

- Learn to say no when appropriate. And stick to it.
- Create consistency with your partner in providing discipline and punishment.
- Have kids participate in volunteer and community work.
- Don't live your life vicariously through theirs.
- Use language you want them to use.
- Build great relationships at work and at home, so they can see how.
- Teach them to make good choices.
- Set parameters so there are consequences for bad behavior and rewards for good behavior.
- Talk about sex and drugs.
- Don't do anything you don't want them to do.
- Teach them the value of money and the importance of earning, saving, and spending it wisely.

Cyberbullying

Cyberbullying is a growing problem for kids. In Chapter 13, we talked about the Internet being used to spread ugly stories about companies. Cyberbullying is the same, except for schoolchildren. It spreads whispers and jeers online through web sites focused on crude insults. There was one example about Kylie, an eighth grader, that was titled "Kill Kylie Incorporated." It began with "Kylie is queer because . . . ," and readers could add their comments in a blog type of format. Kylie eventually changed schools because neither the school nor the parents knew how to put a stop to it.

Kids seem to be encouraged by the anonymity available online, and with a click of a mouse they can engage with a far broader audience. This excruciatingly public humiliation is spread farther and more quickly and can result in lasting emotional damage for the child. Many educators and state legislatures are creating new policies that deal with cyberbullying. So on a personal note, pay attention to what is happening to your kids, and take action when appropriate.

Here is the difficulty. Some teachers and schools are hesitant to approach the children and parents with these problems because they have been told before that it is not their business. Toxic People and children are not a good mix. A toxic situation will influence the behavior of that child forever, not to mention how this disrupts the learning environment.

Decontaminating— Your Personal Responsibility

Al asked me if I was interested in going to Manzanillo, Mexico, to fish for billfish and marlin. "Of course!," I said, because one of my life dreams is to catch a big billfish. Traveling with six other couples was easy, as someone else made the arrangements. When we arrived, I unpacked all our fishing clothes, hats, sunscreen, and shoes. That evening we met in the lobby for dinner. It was a real shock when the lead planner said that there would be a three-day fishing tournament for the "boys," and the "girls" would have one day to fish and that would be the following Wednesday. As I sit here finishing this chapter, it is Tuesday, the day before the girls go fishing, and I leave for Atlanta tomorrow morning. I will miss the fishing in Mexico. I'm not upset, though, because I refuse to be a Toxic Person. I choose to refocus my en-

ergy. Every day has been spent working out, self-indulging myself at the spa, writing, and enjoying the relaxing nonfishing time. There will be plenty of other times for me to fish. Being a pain in the rear is not in the cards.

How would you handle this situation if it happened to you?

Take personal responsibility for your life. I am so tired of people making excuses and resorting to finger-pointing. Look in the mirror right now. Are you happy with what you see? Are you satisfied with your personal and professional life? If you are, congratulations. You are part of the minority. If you are not satisfied, do something about it. Either way, I would recommend rereading this book and applying the ideas to your personal life as well as to your professional life. Perhaps you should get the CDs of this book and listen to them on your commute (see page 222 for information about my web site).

CHAPTER 18

Survivor

▌ ▌ ▌

You have decided to be a survivor instead of a victim of Toxic People. Good for you. Hard work lies ahead, and your habits have to be changed. Use this chapter as a reminder of what you need to focus on to stabilize the changes you want in your life.

Leader Checklist

❏ Hire upbeat people. Training someone in the skill is easier than instilling a positive attitude.
❏ Immediately address employee issues. Otherwise, they will only get worse.

- ❏ Build relationships with everyone.
- ❏ Don't become angry. Stay in control. It's your job.
- ❏ Never show favoritism.
- ❏ Check the perception your people have of you at least annually.
- ❏ Handwrite notes of thanks and acknowledgment.
- ❏ Listen.
- ❏ Celebrate and allow people to have fun.
- ❏ Know people's goals and help them achieve success.
- ❏ Train your people.

Employee Checklist

- ❏ Do your job well.
- ❏ Don't waste time. Your company doesn't pay you to make personal calls or to surf the Internet.
- ❏ Never gossip.
- ❏ Ask for help, especially when prioritizing your tasks.
- ❏ Volunteer, but don't overwhelm yourself.
- ❏ Ask for training. If the company doesn't give it to you, pay for it yourself.
- ❏ Remember "other duties as assigned," and do them gratefully.
- ❏ Work well with everyone, and remember that a co-worker doesn't have to be your best friend.
- ❏ If you don't like your job or boss, leave. Find something you do like.

Survivor Checklist

The real questions are: What will you change? How will you do it? To guarantee health, happiness, and wealth, use the following survivor checklist and Toxic People will never get in your way again!

- ❏ Read and listen to good information.
- ❏ Make first-rate choices.
- ❏ Be open to other people's opinions and thoughts.
- ❏ Figure out what clogs your filter and change it.
- ❏ You don't have to approve. You do have to accept.
- ❏ Don't let the minority rule the majority. Speak up!
- ❏ Build relationships to build profits.
- ❏ Tell your face when you're smiling inside.
- ❏ Give feedback. Use "liked best" and "next time."
- ❏ Invest in yourself. Stop expecting others to take care of you.
- ❏ Be a role model every minute of every day.
- ❏ Take personal responsibility for everything.
- ❏ Take it. Leave it. Change it. What's your plan?
- ❏ Choose to manage conflict well.
- ❏ Manage your money. Lead a simpler life.
- ❏ Everyone you touch is your customer.
- ❏ Take a good look at who you have become.
- ❏ Be flexible.
- ❏ Lighten up.
- ❏ Celebrate everything.

Check my web site at www.MarshaPetrieSue.com for additional tips and tools for managing your life and Toxic People. Your challenge is to apply these survival tactics to manage people who create perplexity, puzzlement, and pandemonium without using weapons or duct tape. Good luck!

Pledge

I, _____ [your name], promise that I will identify toxic behavior, use new skills in my approach, and *never* use excuses again. I have the strength and fortitude to continue to practice, even after I have failed. I am never the Toxic Person. I pledge to stay calm and keep my temper. I promise never to take a Toxic Person's behavior personally or to seek retribution. I know how to keep my power by maintaining control. I create my own environment that nurtures my success. I am the master of my future, my stress level, and my own behavior.

About the Author

Marsha Petrie Sue is the Mohammed Ali of communications. She can dance, look pretty, and she uses the entire ring. Marsha also knows how and when to land a knockout punch. Her information combines charm school with live ammunition. She provides tactics for managing people, employees, and clients that create perplexity, puzzlement, and pandemonium at work and at home. "Let's be honest," she says, "some of the situations you encounter are toxic and you need to learn how to handle it or they'll tear you apart."

Marsha holds a masters degree in Business Administration from the University of Phoenix. She is the author of the award-winning book *The CEO of YOU: Leading Yourself to Success* (Communicating Results Press, 2nd ed., 2002).

Having enjoyed a successful career as an executive with Fortune 100 companies, Marsha is now president of Communicating Results, providing keynotes and presentations to associations and corporations. She is the recipient of the Women of Spirit Award from the American Red Cross and Morton's, which was awarded in recognition of her continued volunteerism and community work.

Marsha and her husband Al live in Scottsdale, Arizona, and get away from the killer summer heat by retreating to their cabin in the Arizona White Mountains. They are birders and love hiking and fishing. In addition, Marsha enjoys photography and golf.

About the Author

Marsha's DVDs, CDs, and audio recordings are from her live presentations as well as studio recording sessions. Visit her web site at www.MarshaPetrieSue.com for additional resources and for booking information. To reach Marsha,

E-mail: Information@MarshaPetrieSue.com

Or call toll-free: 1-866-661-8756 or 480-661-8756